M
I
S
S
I
S
S
I
P
P
I

the imperishable quiet at the heart of form

— Theodore Roethke

Mississippi

Poems by
Ann Fisher-Wirth

Photographs by
Maude Schuyler Clay

WingsPress
San Antonio, Texas
2018

Mississippi © 2018 by Wings Press for Ann Fisher-Wirth and Maude Schuyler Clay
Cover photograph and all interior photographs by Maude Schuyler Clay. Used by permission of the artist.

ISBN: 978-1-60940-560-1 (Cloth/hardback)

E-books:
ePub: 978-1-60940-561-8
Mobipocket/Kindle: 978-1-60940-562-5
Library PDF: 978-1-60940-563-2

Wings Press
627 E. Guenther
San Antonio, Texas 78210
Phone/fax: (210) 271-7805
On-line catalogue and ordering:
www.wingspress.com

Wings Press books are distributed to the trade by
Independent Publishers Group • www.ipgbook.com
PRINTED IN CHINA

Library of Congress Cataloging-in-Publication Data:

Names: Fisher-Wirth, Ann, author. | Clay, Maude Schuyer, photographer.
Title: Mississippi / poems by Ann Fisher-Wirth ; photographs by Maude Schuyler Clay.

Description: San Antonio, Texas : Wings Press, [2018].
Identifiers: LCCN 2017005581| ISBN 9781609405601 (hardcover : alk. paper) | ISBN 9781609405618 (ePub ebook) | ISBN 9781609405625 (kindle/mobipocket ebook) | ISBN 9781609405632 (library pdf)
Classification: LCC PS3606.I79 A6 2018 | DDC 811/.6--dc23
LC record available at https://lccn.loc.gov/2017031775

Except for fair use in reviews and/or scholarly considerations, no portion of this book may be reproduced in any form without the written permission of the author, photographer, or the publisher.

This book was made possible by generous subvention grants from the University of Mississippi, Oxford, and the Black Earth Institute.

Contents

Foreword

In her recent memoir, *The Faraway Nearby*, the environmental writer Rebecca Solnit writes: "A place is a story, and stories are geography, and empathy is first of all an act of imagination, a storyteller's art, and then a way of traveling from here to there." Mississippi, where I have lived for the past thirty years, suffers from severe environmental degradation that cannot be separated from its history of poverty and racial oppression. Yet the state also possesses great natural beauty and a rich and complex culture, one interwoven from the many voices that have made up its identity. *Mississippi* explores both this degradation and this beauty.

I have come to understand these poems as explorations of voice in its Mississippi plenitude and variety. Recently on Facebook, someone snarkily commented that though we hear people say things like *might could* and *aks*, "That's not English." I completely disagree. I honor the voices, no matter whose they are, both white and African American. I love the rich orality of Mississippi culture, and have tried to express it. To write these poems, I listen to the voices and I listen to Maude's photographs. Out of silence, the poems emerge.

—Ann Fisher-Wirth

M
I
S
S
I
S
S
I
P
P
I

Between two worlds
the soul floats

nothing remains

but purple flowers smeared across the trees
a silver boat tucked in against the bank
the fecund pond like greenish velvet

splotches of light
the whole known world

hollow that boat
empty
but be
still
almost as if
you could walk on the water

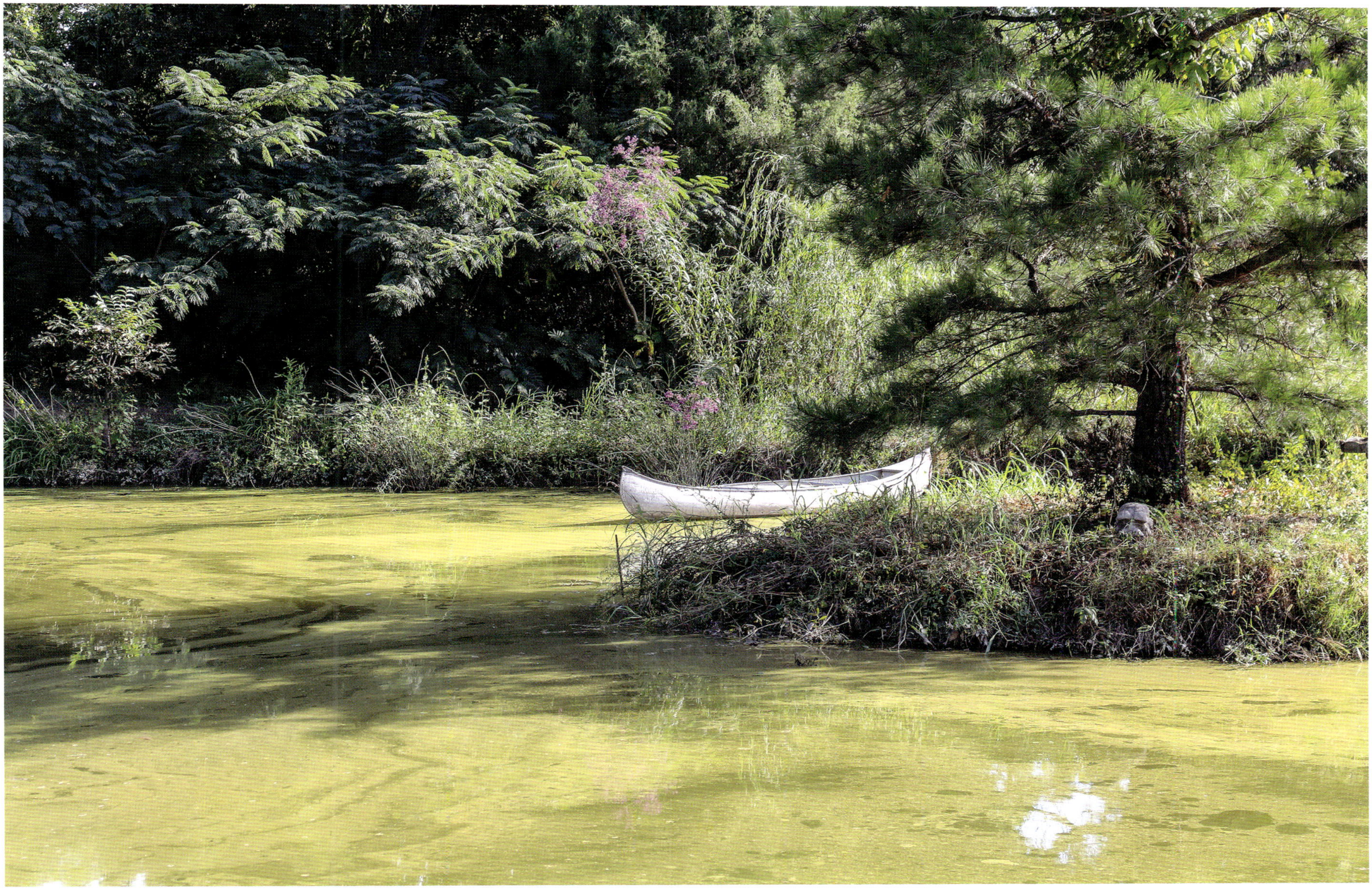

The heron he come from beyond
like a messenger bird
he stand hours fishing in the one spot
I wonder what he be thinking

he be like my grandpa
back in the day
grandpa stand hours fishing in the one spot
never could tell what he be thinking

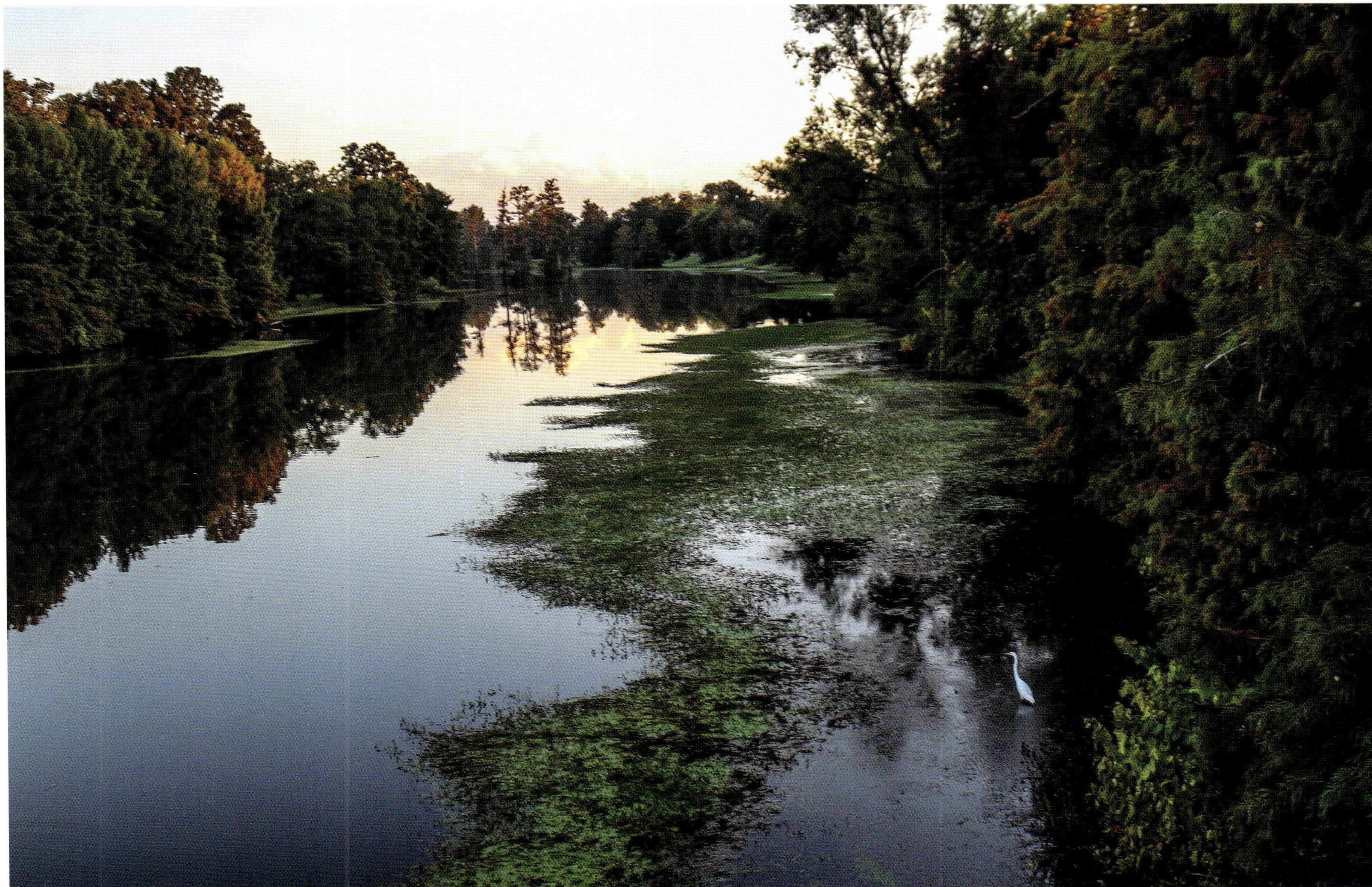

You may not have these cushions
they are the ones my dying aunt chose for me

you may not have these spoons
though they tarnish in my drawer

or the blankets
that I mended

look at this pretty blue plate
with the flowers
and the bird
look at this cast iron skillet

oh, go ahead rise up

smear the boards
soak the house

until it buckles until it cracks

and *whoosh*

with a sigh and *lip* *lip* *lip*
it subsides

Don't you know we'll get away
don't you know we'll leave by boat

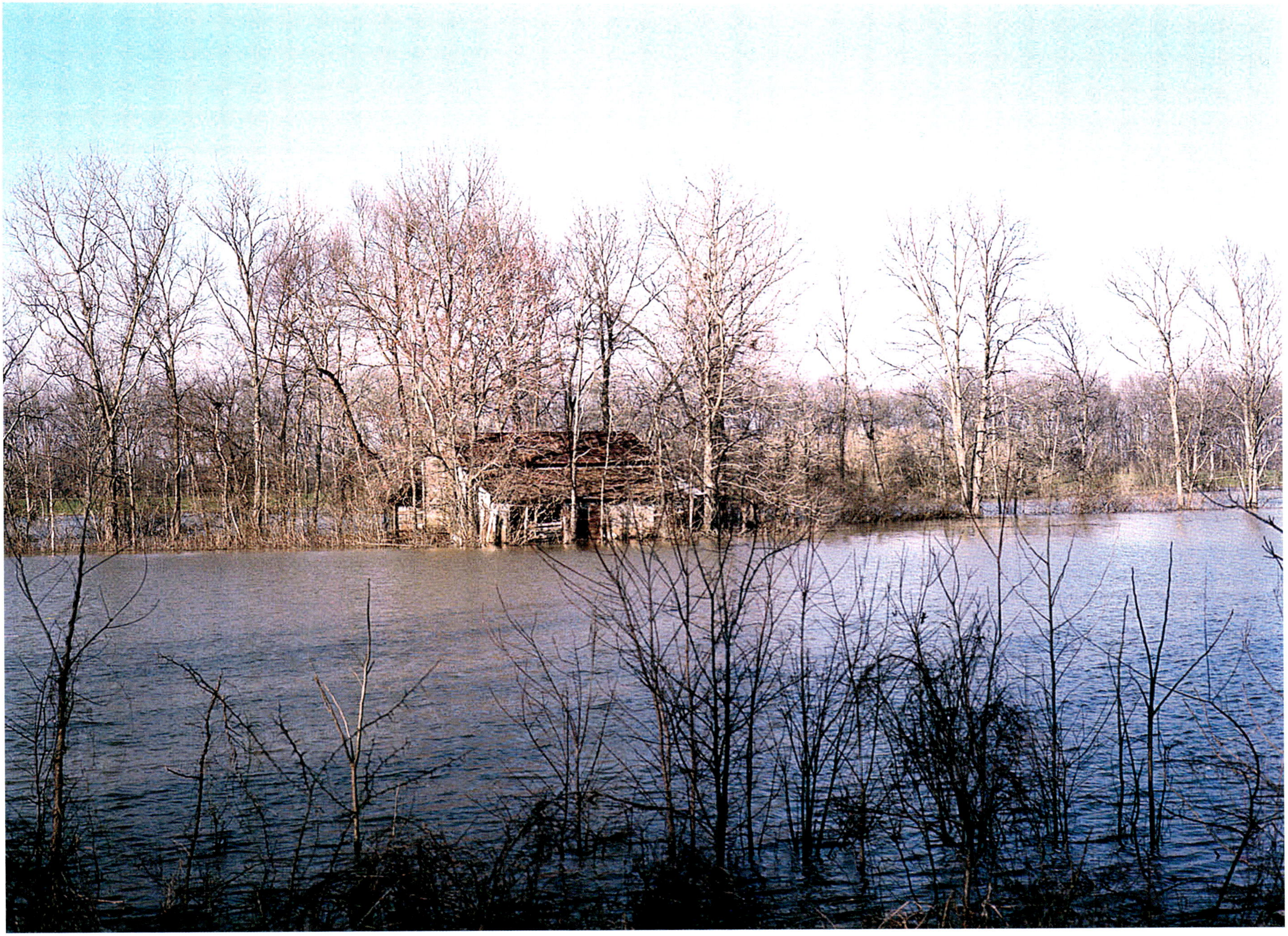

He comes to your door
raw-boned bare-knuckled
looking for anything
rake your driveway wash your windows
offers to chop wood cut grass *ma'am* soft-voiced
anything

and he gets to telling
how like the badger
I burrowed me a place

how he sets his clothes and tools
the jar of nails the saw
his blue-handled hammer
along a bench he built in the hillsides

and tucks his sheets
smooths *the Bear Paw quilt*
my meemaw made it's hard
to keep things off the dirt
but he doesn't mind the baby spiders
them little white things in a filmy cloud
near the door

He tells you about the bluetick hound
the horse he had as a kid
the job he wants to get mopping floors
stocking shelves at the Jitney

He rakes takes pay
doesn't want food
drinks a glass of water
ma'am I got what I need in the earth

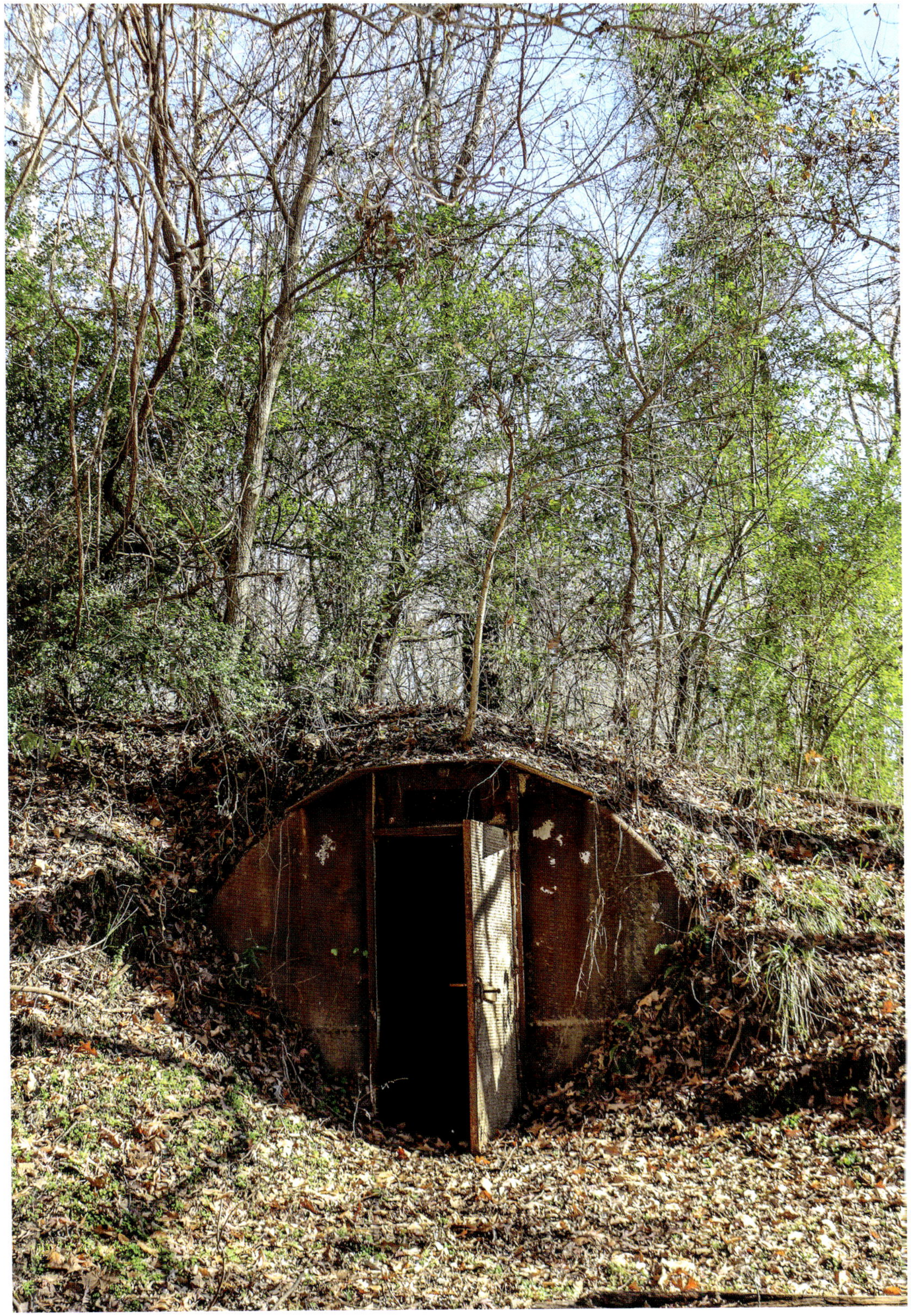

Had me a dog once deep chest
brindle coat
by the looks of it a fine strong dog
but the damn dog wouldn't hunt

would just stand there looking at me

and I don't need to be feeding
no dog that won't hunt you know what I mean?

cute when they come off the mamma
but they got to have that inclination

give em a season it don't work out leave em behind
you know what I mean?

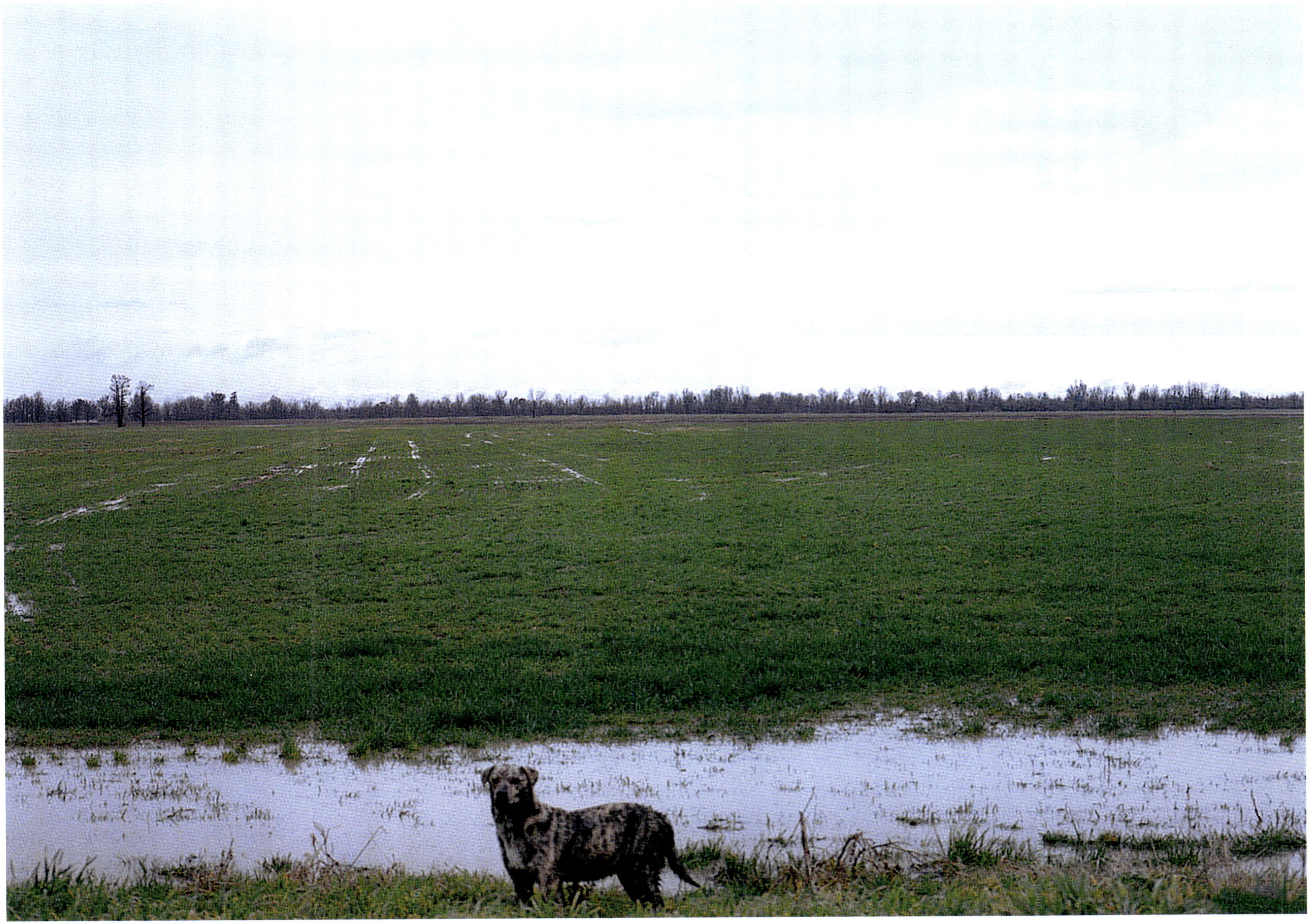

Women what do they want

she's always hanging pictures of the ocean
when we got a nice house
here in town

hardwood floors Jacuzzi big magnolias in the back
the whole 9 yards

and if she tells me again
how her daddy give her an opal ring
how she lost it at the beach
prayed all night to find it

and next day
just running her hands through the sand
there it was

her daddy always her daddy
and his little fishing boat

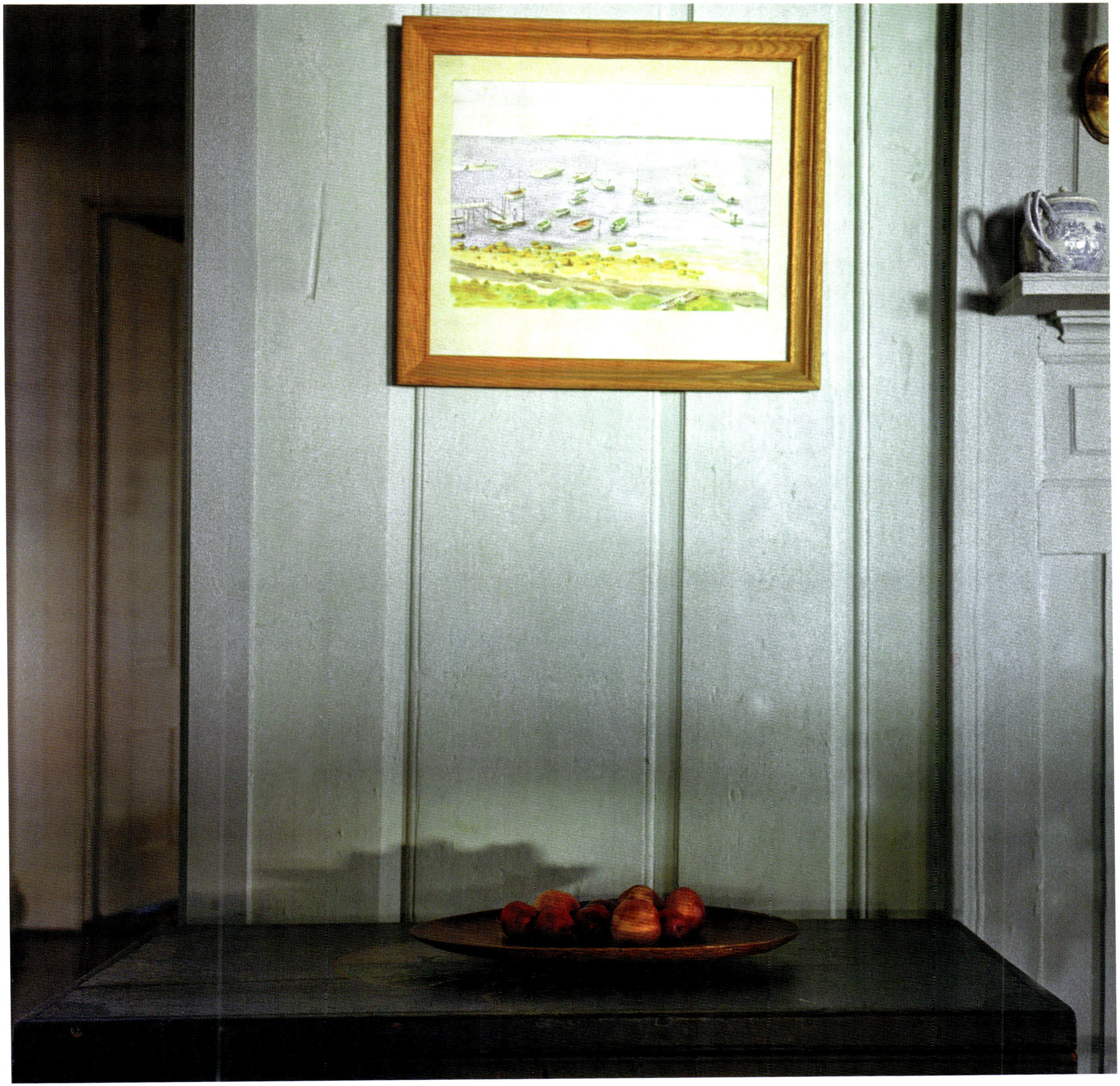

—Then lumbering across the field
crowding their big faces
against the fence
there came a passel of cattle

jammed against their mothers' legs
sweet calves looking up at me
I would like to be a cow
and suckle my babies in a field
until they were taken away from me
I know it's cruel
what they do to calves
but cows don't have to
bail their babies out in the middle
of the night they don't have to
endure the whispering or fight
with their children
or lie awake at 3 a.m. and pray

today we left our daughter at rehab
on a hilltop here in Massachusetts
last chance the judge said
to keep her out of juvie in Mississippi

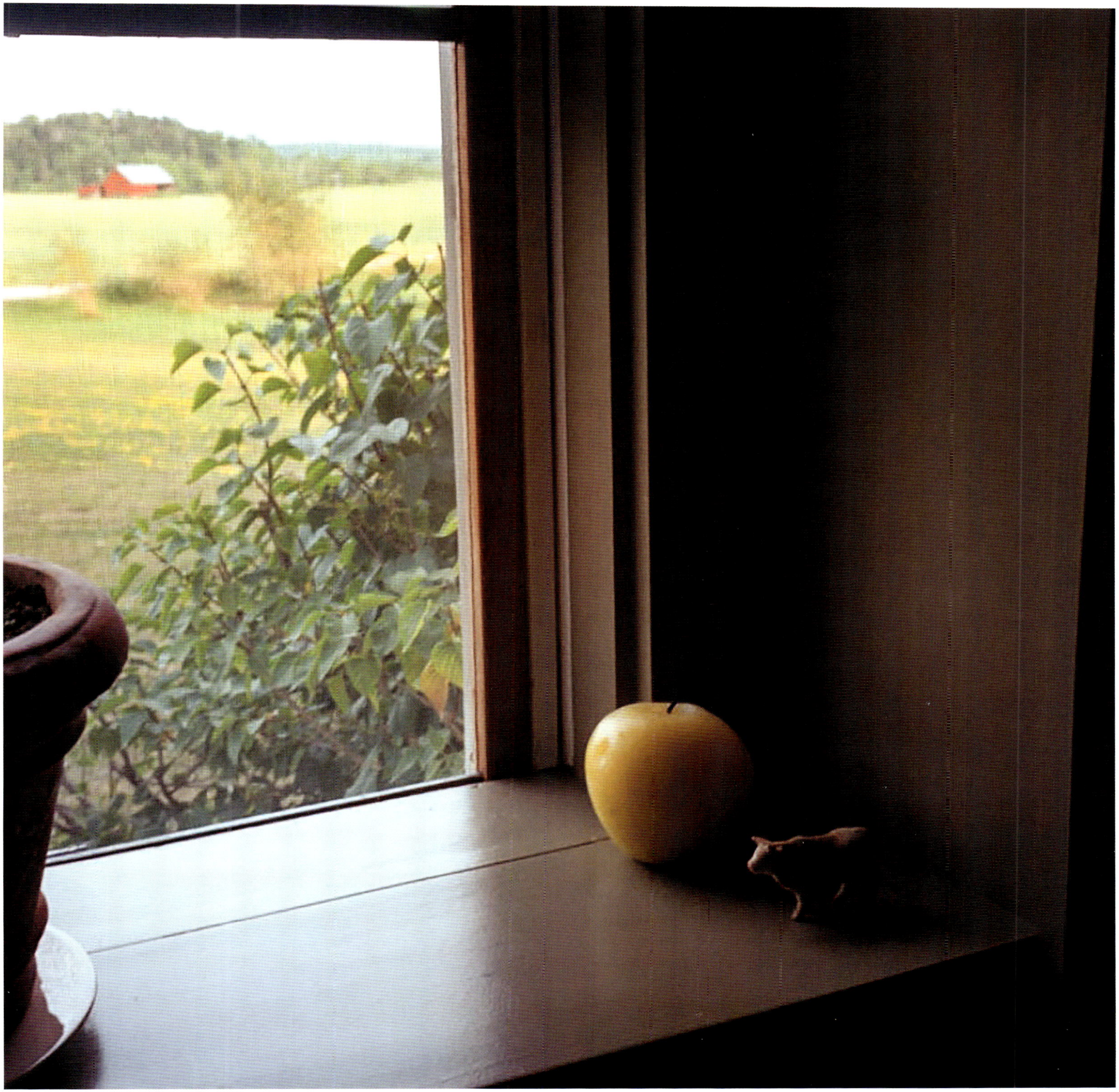

These August afternoons even the candles
melt   dear God   I shape them again with my hands

stay there

but the wax just sweats and oozes
there on the mantel
next to mama's painting

Sometimes I lie on the floor's wide planks

too tired   too listless to move

as all day the sun
swims from right to left across the window

Once when she was dying
mama saw a dog   or thought she saw a dog
beneath the pecan trees in the rain

it turned toward her she said
and then it disappeared

mostly she slipped
in and out   in and out   and deeper

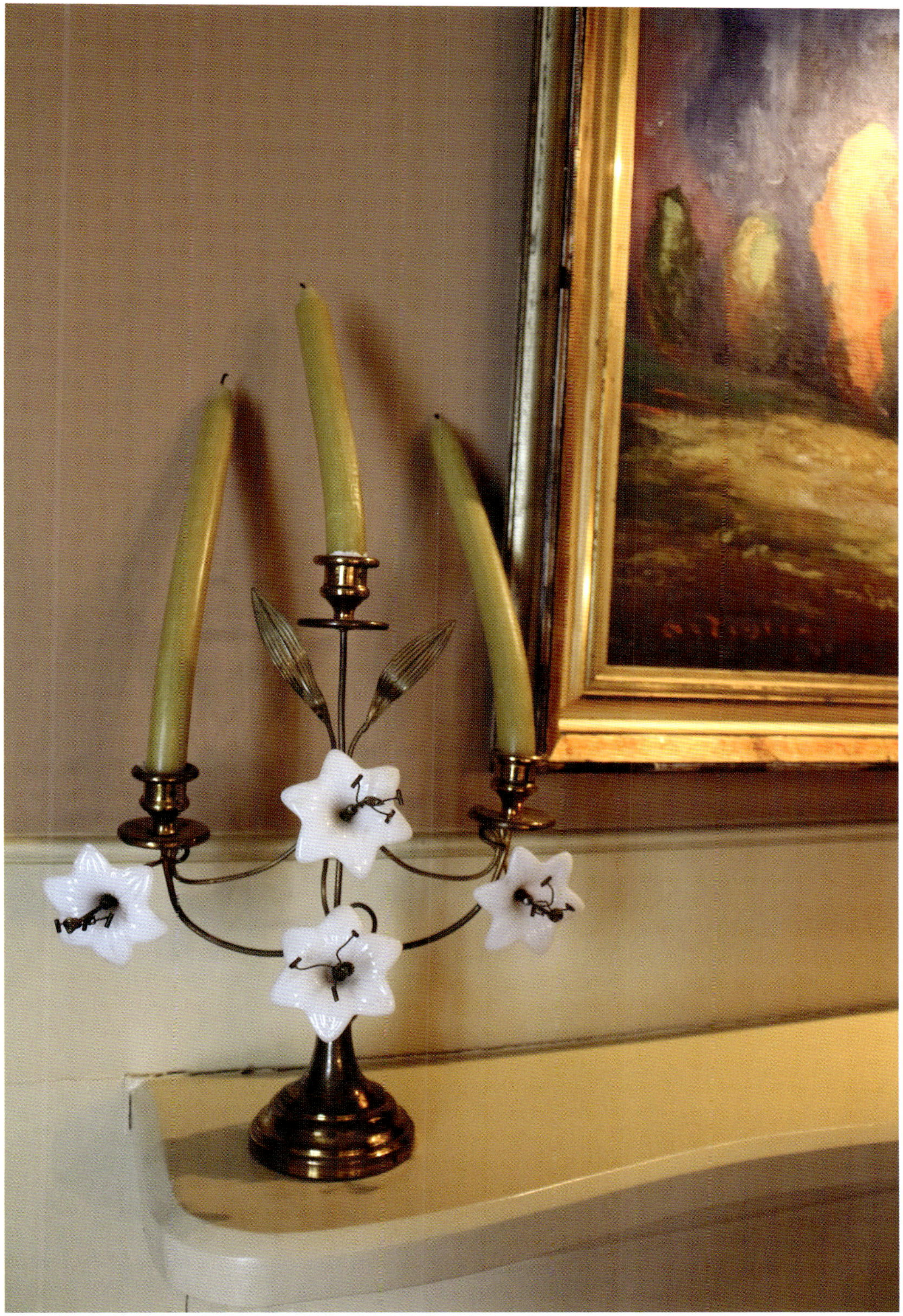

That's me in my new silk blouse
raising my arms to fix my hair

my husband called me Goldilocks
said I made everything golden

(whisper a little secret
it's a spray paint trick I learned at school)

horses? we always had horses
Mr. Bobo
mama's Mist o'the Glen
and the sweetest little Shetland
my daughter named
Princess Shalimar

our life together was always the best
best food best house
best people

my husband Donnie built our church
at Christmas we hosted 200

and once *Vogue* magazine
photographed
my hands

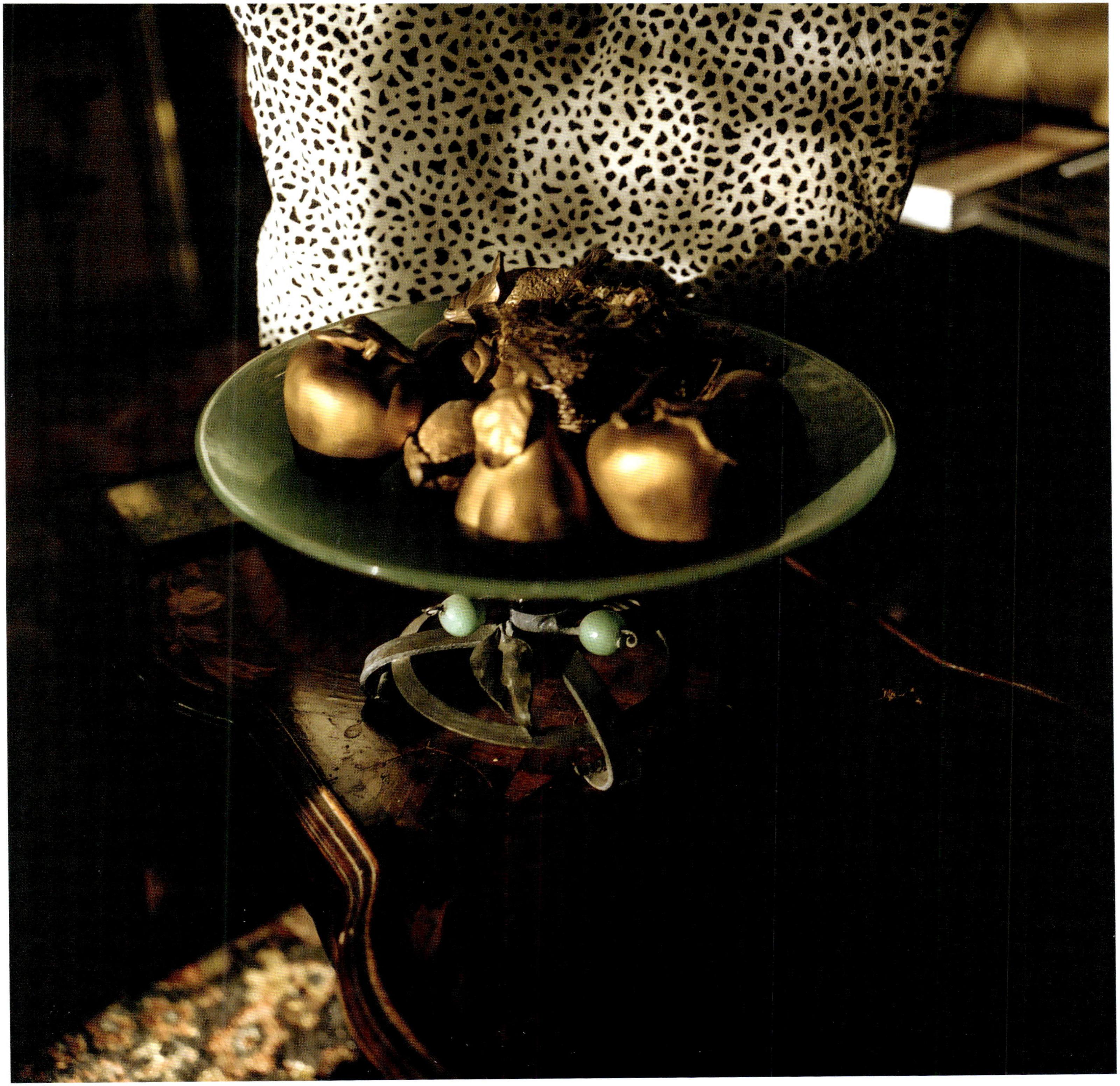

I said *write me, Jig Jig.*
I'm taking the Greyhound to Memphis
to visit my camp friend Shirley.
We'd been dating three weeks.
For Easter he give me a kitty bank
and a flat of purple pansies.
So I told him what to write, give him a little kiss,
and then I'm gone. I missed his fuzzy chin,
how he'd bid for my lunch box
when all the girls brought lunches
to social dancing.
                Then after I got back,
here comes the letter he'd sent to Memphis,
all the way back to Tula. Opened it
all pittypat but what a disappointment.
Your eyes are like lakes, your cheeks are
like ruby pettals, and it went on and on,
just the way I told him. Signed it, too,
the way I told him, scrumptious word
I got from my uncle's sexy books.
Love, your immorata J. J. Mooney.
Had to dump him after that. Jig Jig
dumb as an egg. Me with my literary future.

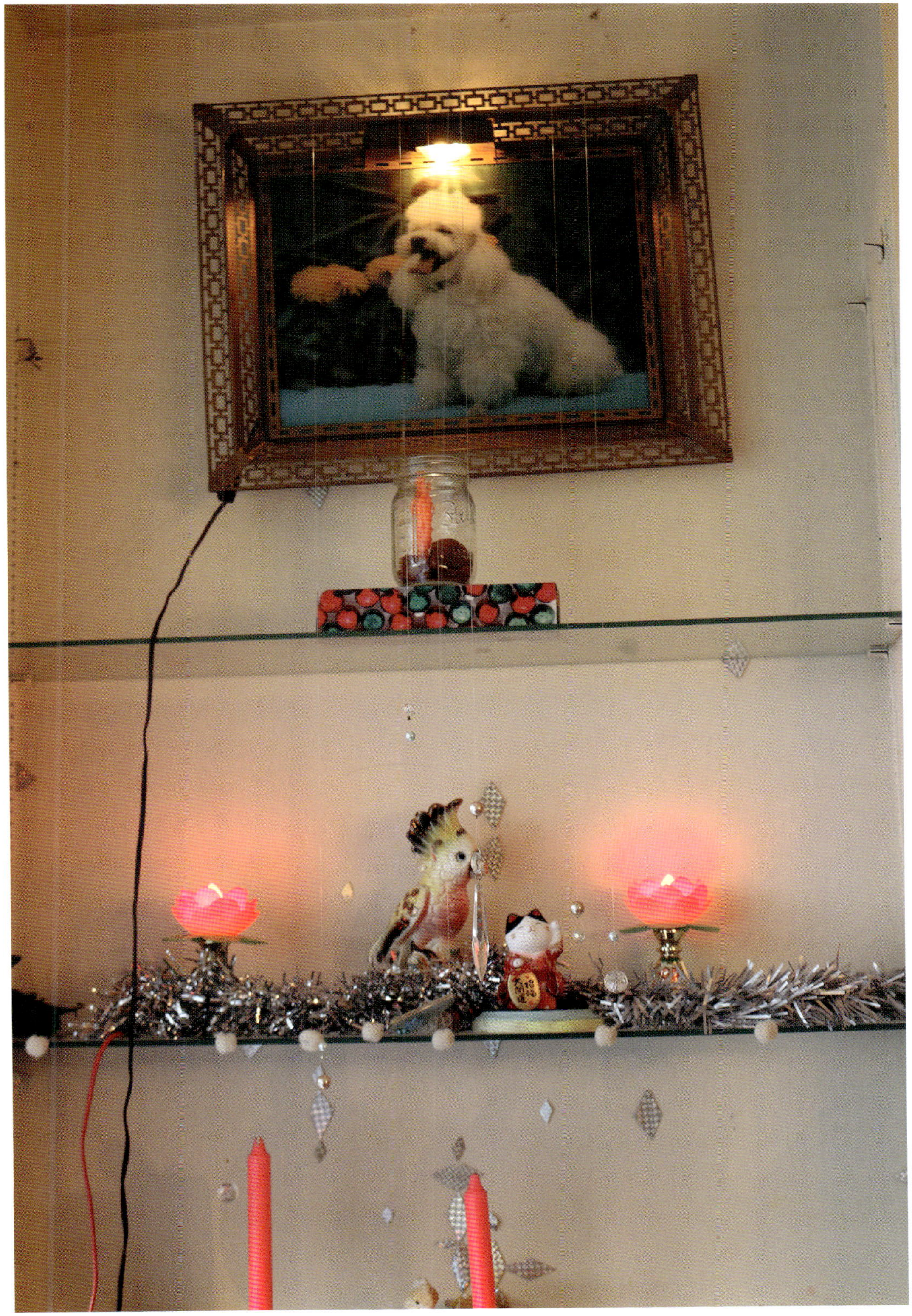

We're mostly headed for hell now the devil's come among us. No point reading the papers, watching the news, just got to lay up for the family best I'm able. My third wife, Jeanie, she's got this little girl, bucktooth as a chipmunk, needs some orthodontia. Wood's rotten on the porch, like to be some job getting that replaced. Squirrels at the wiring in the attic. And I still got to be paying child support to the deep-dyed bitch who run me out, and the other one, Bonnie, good Christian woman, good cook too, but she didn't take to doin the dirty. Well what do you think?—couldn't help it none after Jeanie leaned over me, holding my jaw while the doc pulled that molar. Soil's poor, too much rain, no rain, cotton used to be good, but sparse this year no matter how you spray it—and now I'm up against selling off more timber. Loblolly pine. Grows fast, good money, but even it don't thicken like it used to. Heart pine? thing of the past. Can't find that good hard sappy wood no more, it's all cut down, like my grandma's house was built of, even the termites couldn't chew it.

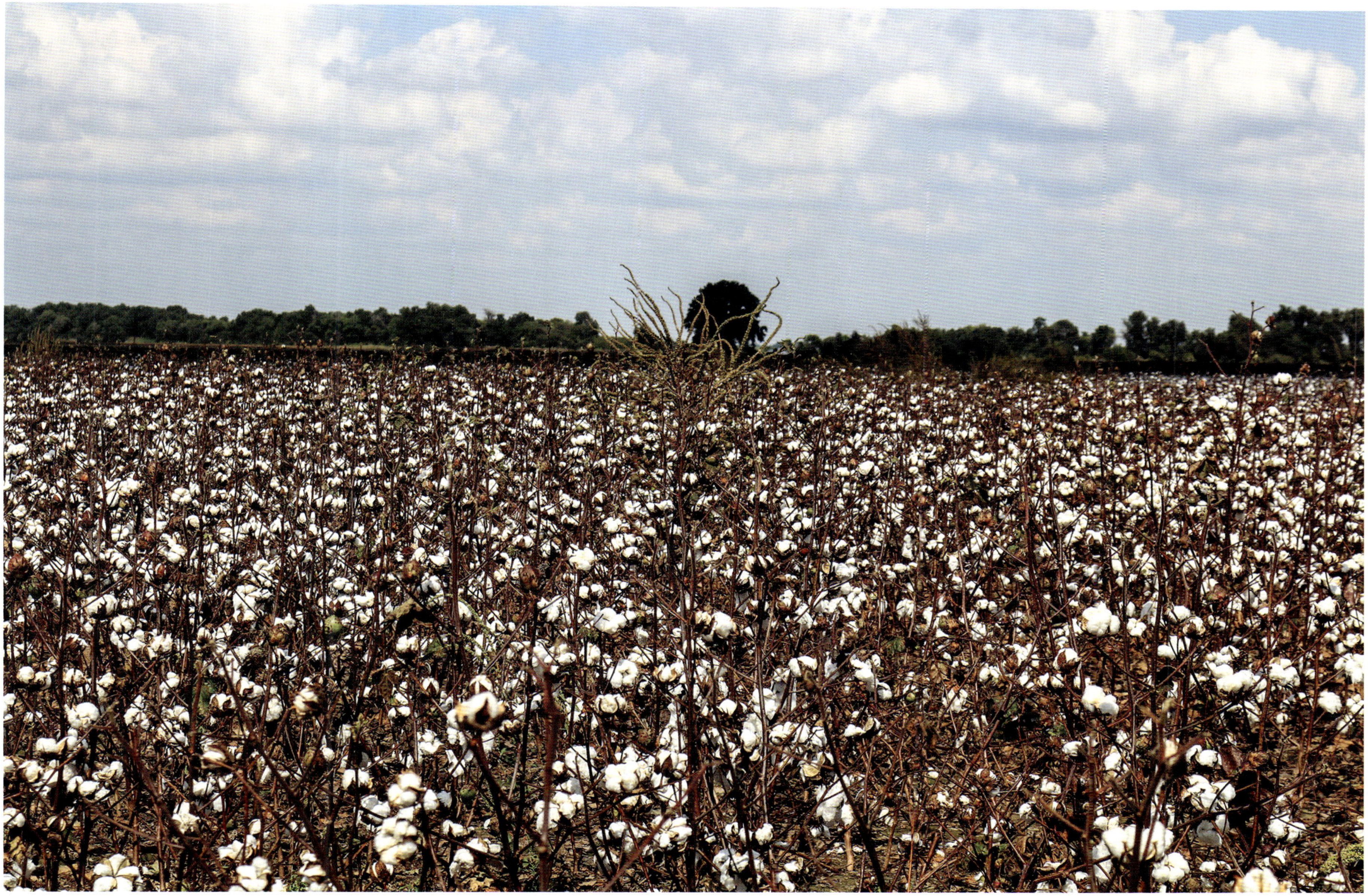

Pardon my French my mamma drives
me apeshit. All these questions. Who
was there what did I eat who did I dance
with what were the other girls wearing
did they compliment my hair my dress
my shoes did I have a good time? And
Lord Lord I can hardly breathe when she
starts on hold your spine straight honey
lamb don't roll your shoulders carry
your head high so what if you haven't
developed where girls want to develop
I promise you six ways to Sunday you'll
fill out in time. Just got to keep you pure
and sweet a petal-fresh and upstanding
girl a man would want to marry. Well
a girl's entitled to a little privacy but yes
I tell her they loved my dress I danced
every dance and Mikey tried to kiss me
in the kitchen. She squeals. I certainly
hope you slapped him she says. She'd
believe *that* she'd believe anything
but anything to get her off my back.

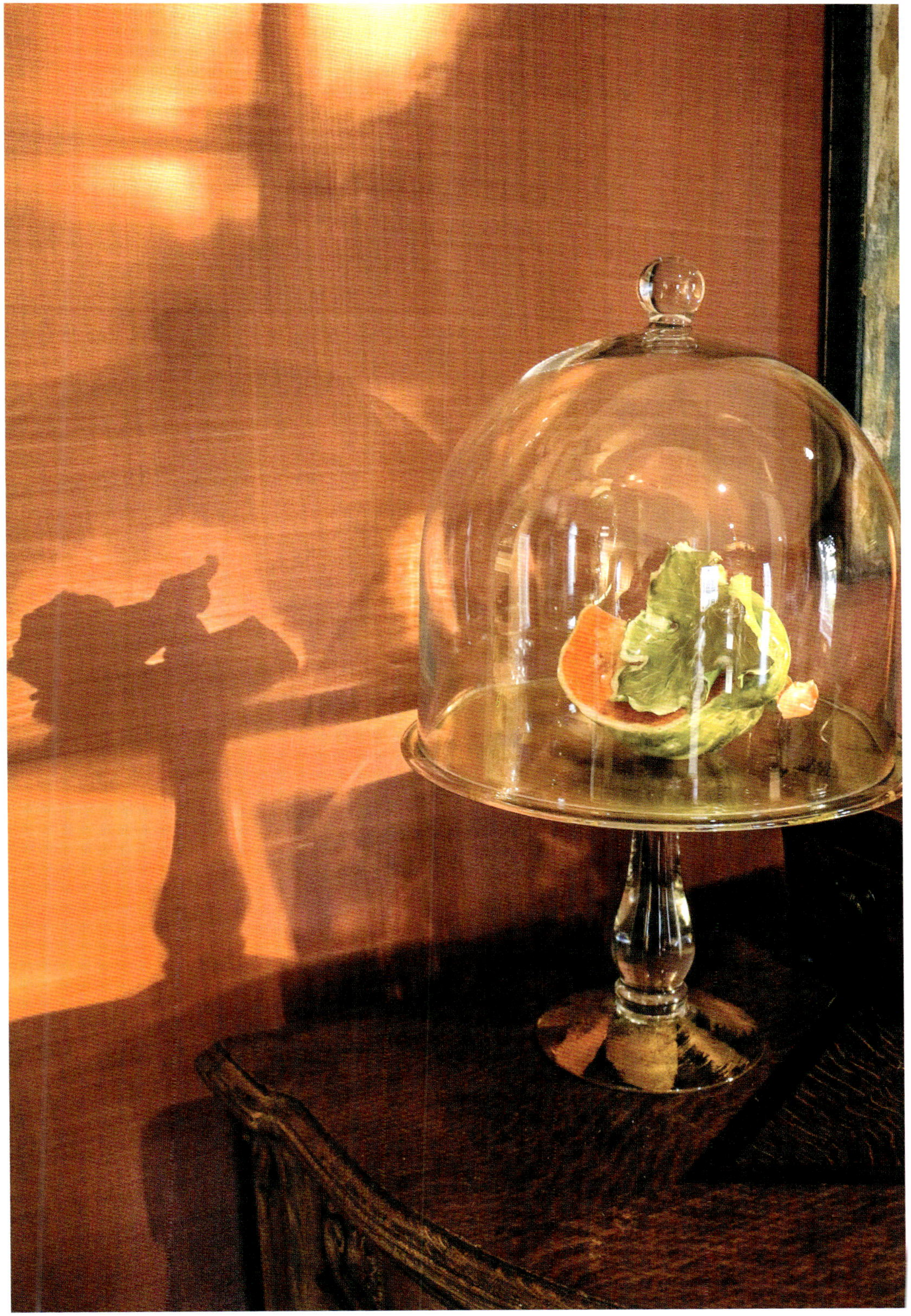

We read these books in 101
this old guy poke his eyes out

and then there's this war between
a couple a brothers and then

this other old guy
say Angon you goin in a cave to die

if you mess with buryin that body

and the teacher aks what we do
if we was Angon

I tell her   No way in hell Id let them
vulchers eat my brother

no ma'am Id do just like Angon done
my daddy my brother my cusin all them

not meat in the rode for vulchers
shoot me   see if I care

put me in one them caves
Angon was right

family the only thing that matters

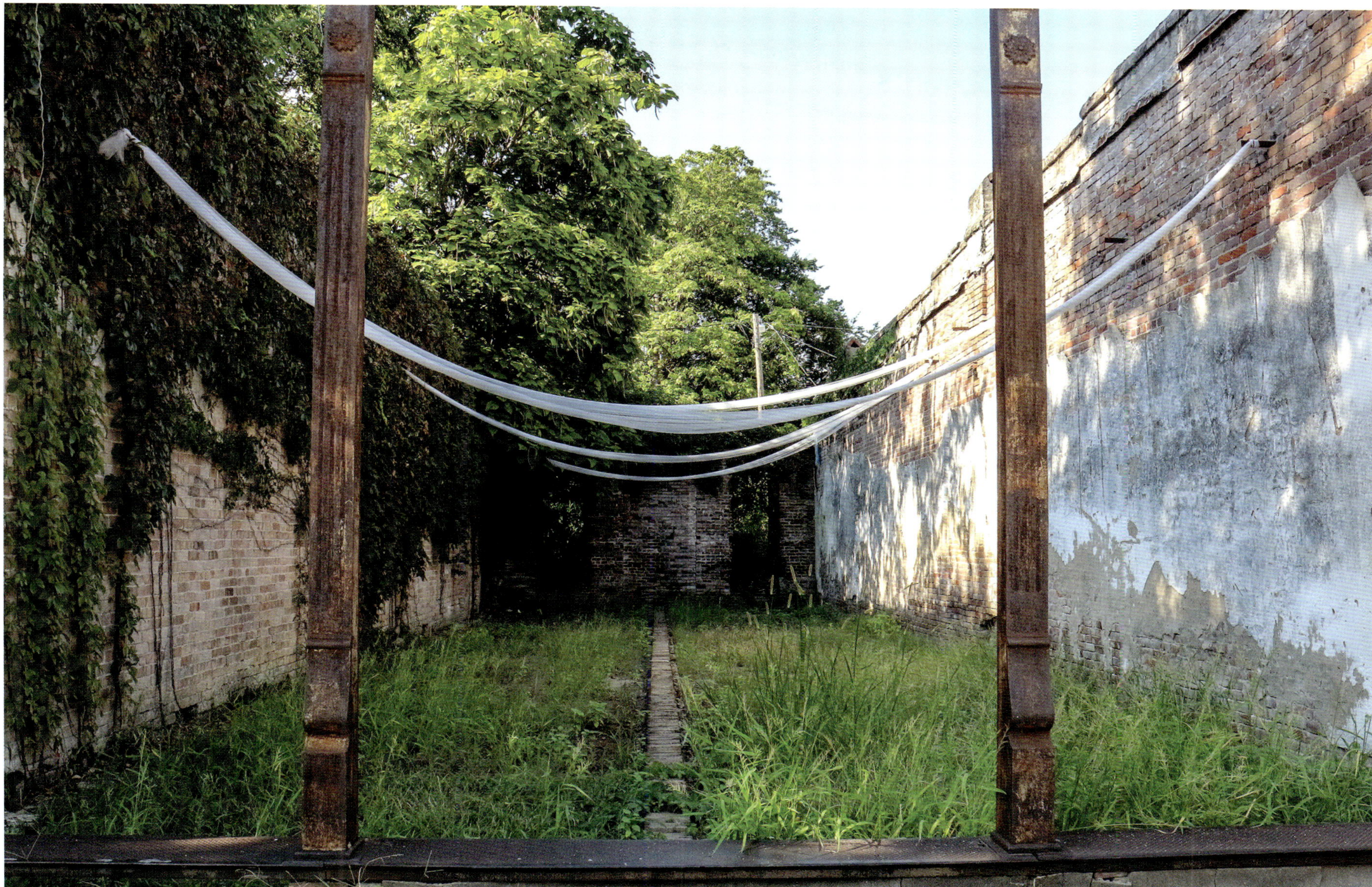

I won Miss Physical Processes,
whatever *that* means. I was never
so embarrassed, riding along
on the back of that pink Chevy
doing the wave *flip* *flip* goes the hand,
and grinning, Jesus, waving
and grinning at Nana and Papa
and all the little cousins who come
to watch me in the homecoming parade.
I put Vaseline on my teeth
so my lip wouldn't get stuck, that's how
they do on TV in the pageants. Look,
how I see it, I'll be spending my life
ringing up sales at Walgreen's.
Nobody ever gets out of here.
So this was my big weekend and then
oh Lord *woosh* here it comes,
blood on my turquoise satin ball gown
I bought for the occasion at Lester's
for Ladies up in Grenada. Miss Physical
Processes, that's me I guess, and I
wish to hell I'd never been a beauty queen.

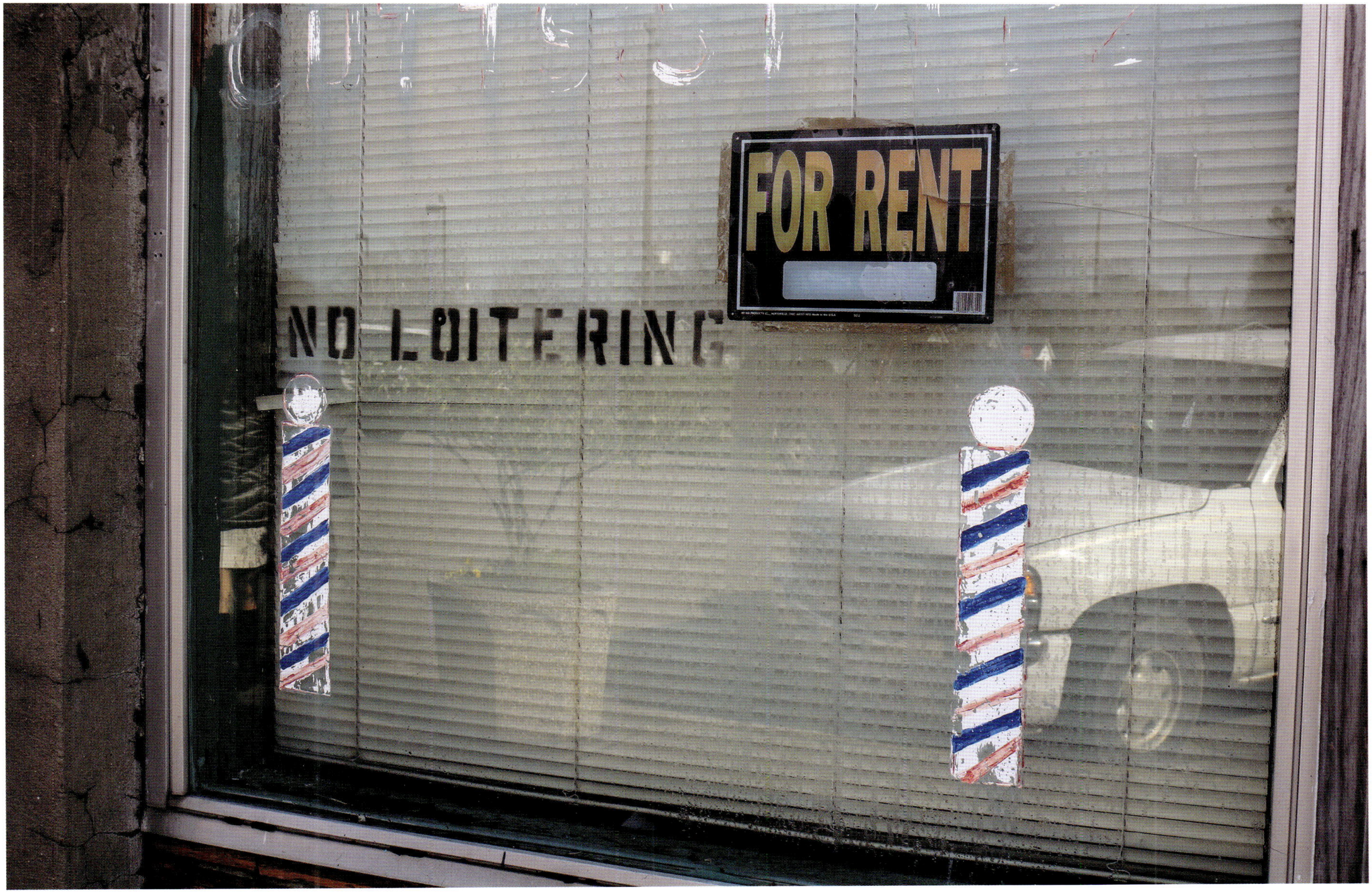
FOR RENT
NO LOITERING

Well *of course* we don't condone
underage drinking but neither
do we condone the country police
who put up speed traps to catch the boys
with nicer cars. What's the good
of setting a black mark on their futures?
And hasn't your own son, too,
been to the top of Sam Fool Hill?
I was never so embarrassed in my life
as when a phone call came
one midnight—some woman saying
that, crazed with beer,
our Mikey had run his car in a ditch,
shot out her mailbox,
and nearly killed her cat.
Oh heavens, only with BBs. Fortunately,
we know the judge, Big Mike and he
were at school together. You love
your sons so much when they're little,
and then when they get older
and their nature starts inciting them,
what are they supposed to do with all that wild?

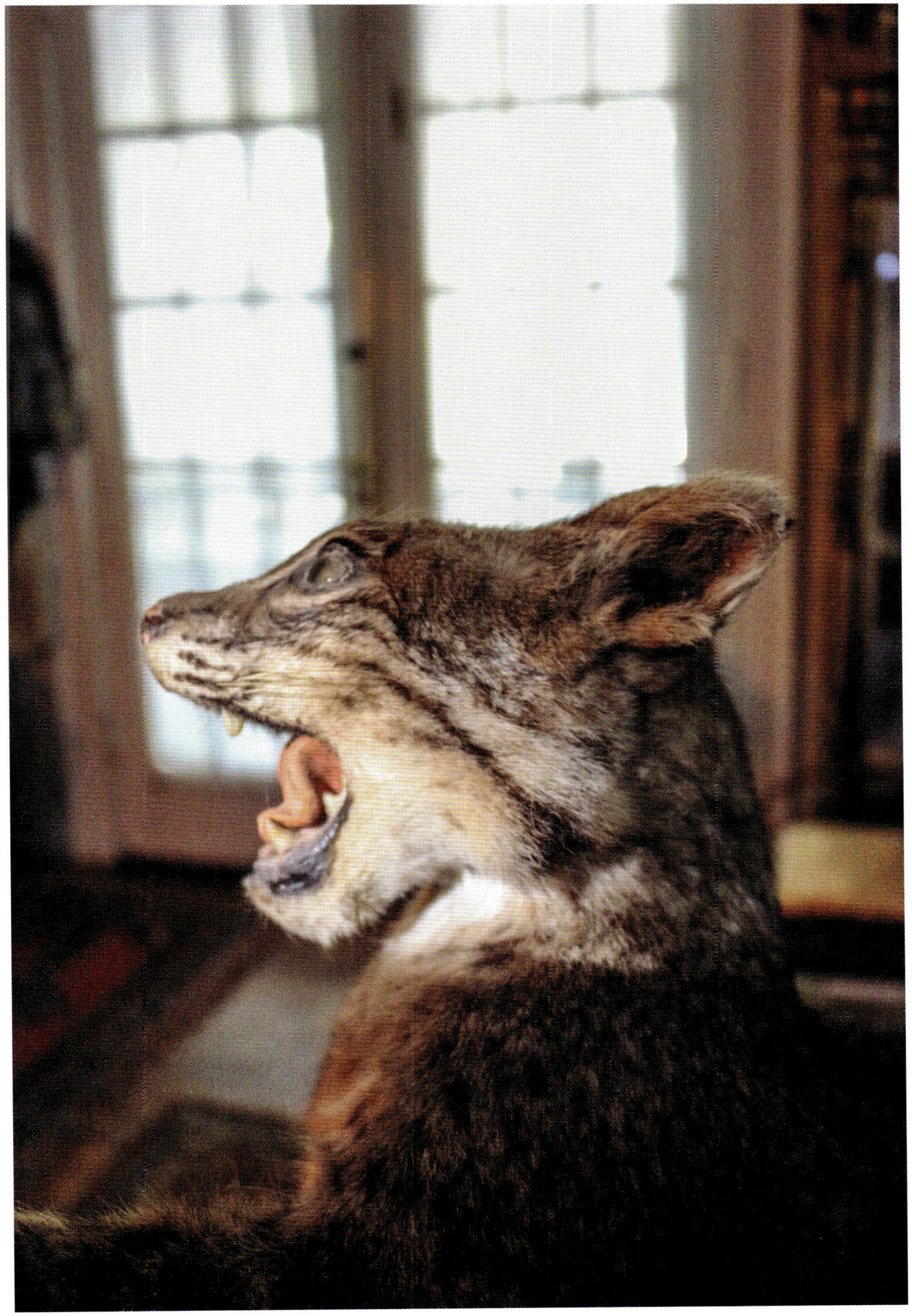

Sister Laurent made us memorize
L'art
est toujours un vol
de la réalité

Which she said can be uttered only in French
because *vol*
is both *theft* and *flight*

and I have not forgotten Sister Laurent
or Our Lady Academy
the rustle of pages
the clock slowly ticking

so now in her blessed memory
I have stolen these pears
and these nectarines
from the ripening trees

and arranged them
for your flight

into a world
where soft clouds bar the sky
and swallows swoop
and twitter
over the gleaming river

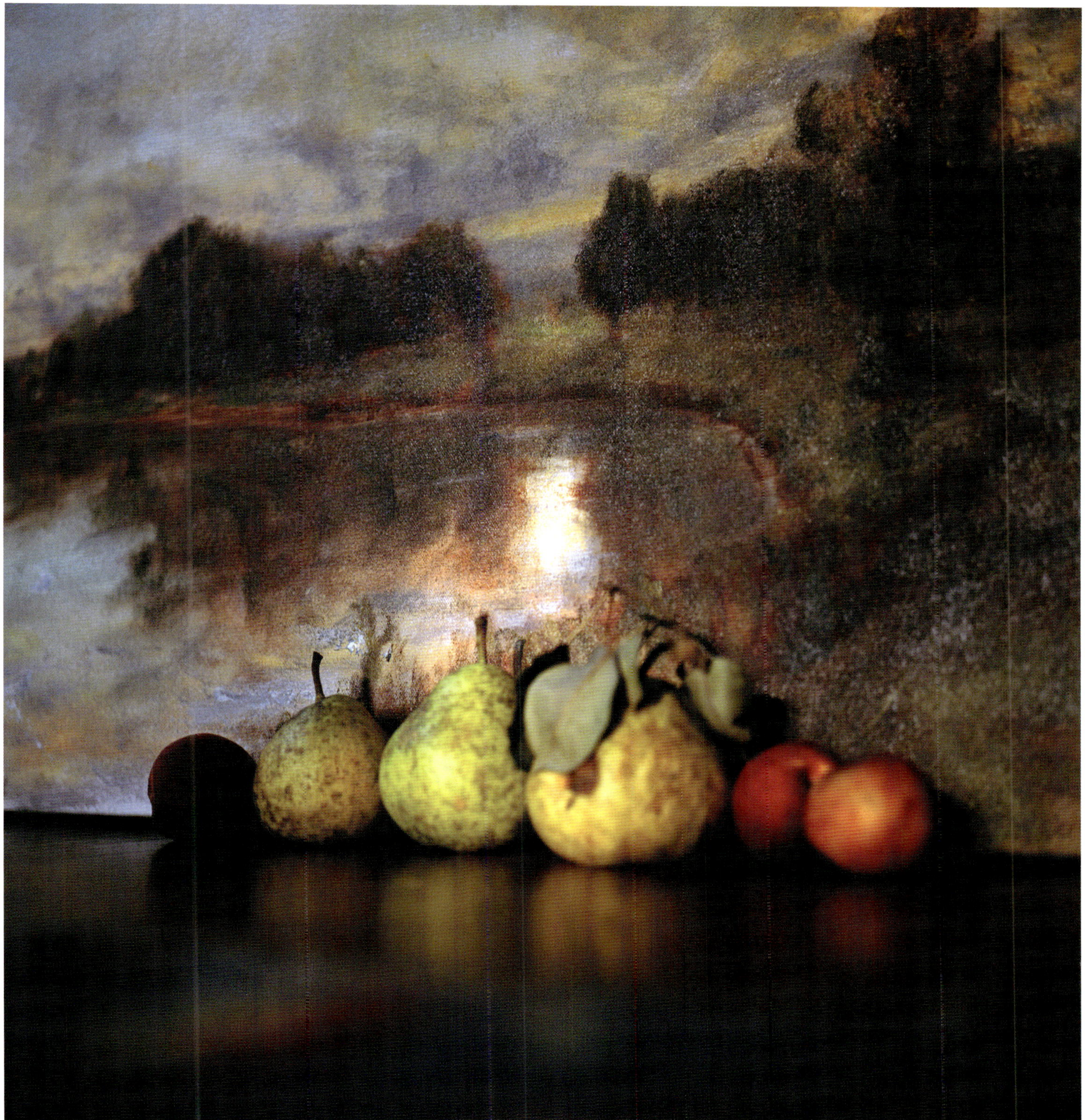

Sometimes I gaze at this
print on my desk
the rough bowl the marble fruit
a thin line bisecting the veined
orange and white melon or apple

then I lose myself
in the oblong reflections
where light glows through a window
in the calmness of wood
the quietness of the room

and consider how that line
on the marble fruit is like the scar
that stitches my belly
from the time I nearly died

how print and marble are not flesh
but I am flesh

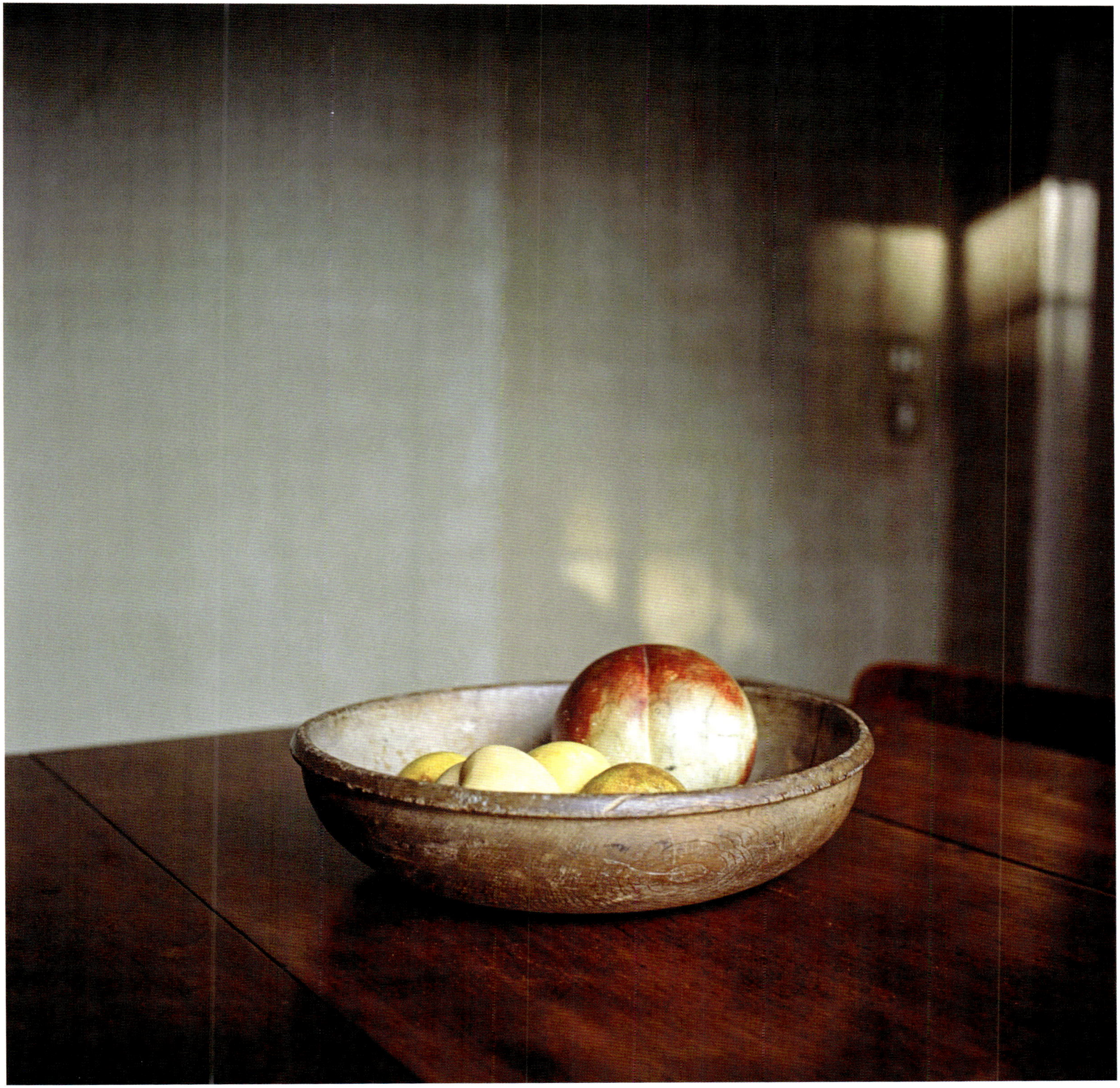

This guy from Berlin came to our school
Episcopal Day
to teach on an art exchange
and he asked me to stay after to photograph me he said
I had the cheekbone like Monica Vitti that's how he said it
you have the cheekbone like Monica Vitti

When he was turning my face this way and that to find
the best light I let him brush his arm across me

I've dated but they were children compared
to the artist from Berlin with his
green eyes his
bracelet of tattoos and spiky hair

I'm in love that's why I feel strange not to mention
after he left this stupid school was boring as ever

and oh my God my parents
make me go to cotillion

He gave the principal this signed photograph when I
see it every time swear to God my body burns now

I'm going to Germany next year till then
I just lay out I don't want to do anything just wrap up in my blanket
and lay out

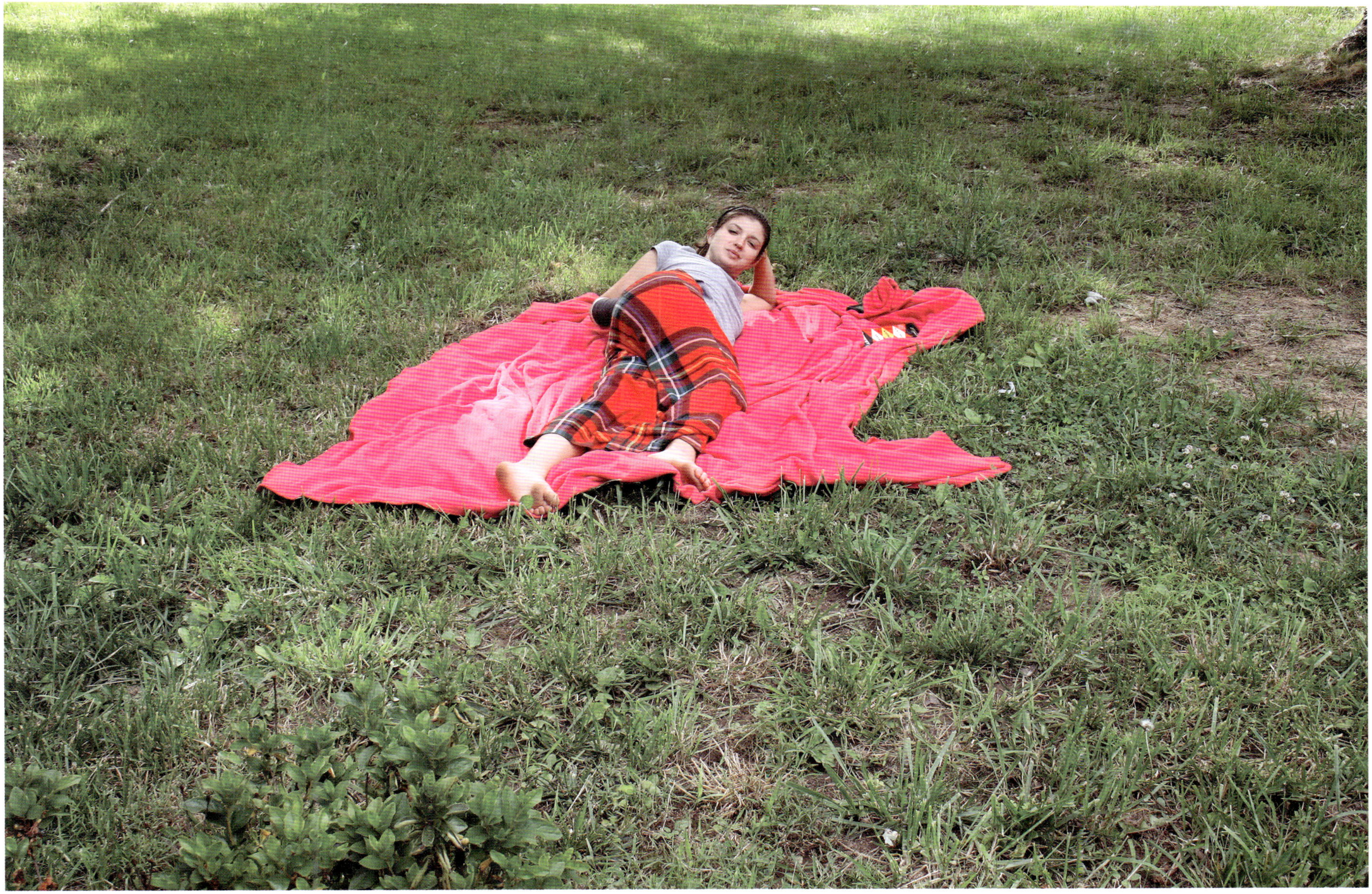

—And the five o'clock sun
on the glass-front bookcase
where once I crouched to read my father's Tennyson

I hope to see my Pilot face to face
when I have crost the bar

mother napping daddy not home yet
just such a light as today

(but Tennyson said
in the dark I have not seen him)

now they are gone
mother daddy my sister Virginia

Why do I save their things
damask napkins
I was hemming
for Virginia
mother's majolica plate
now piled with fruit
the curved chairs the gleaming table

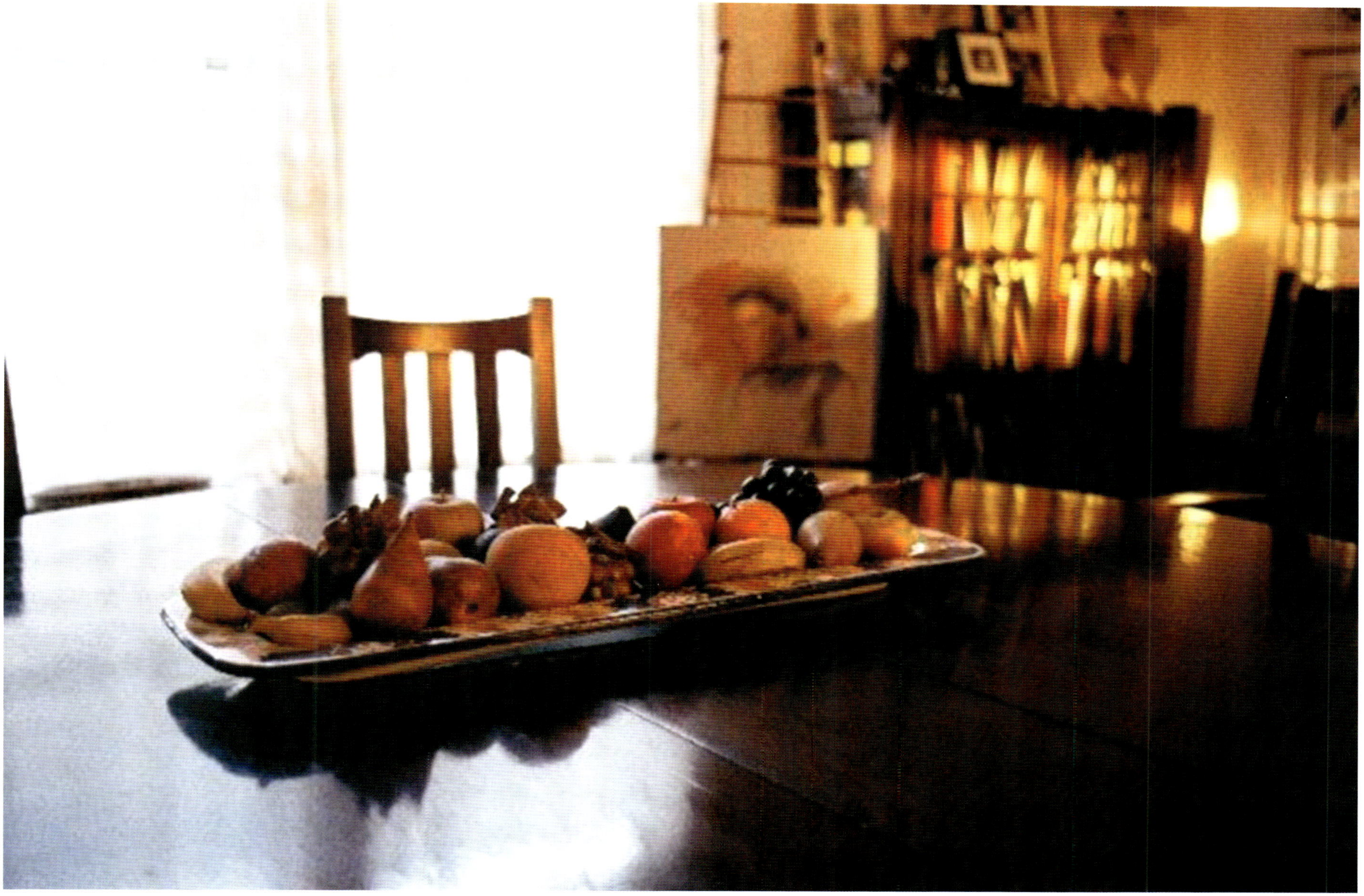

You stand in Tree, *vrksasana*,
as the quiet self blossoms

downward into the waters

beautiful dancer
all around the rose-light flows

summer's final insects trill

the grasses flourish upward
beyond, the open lake

and the hills unfold their darkness

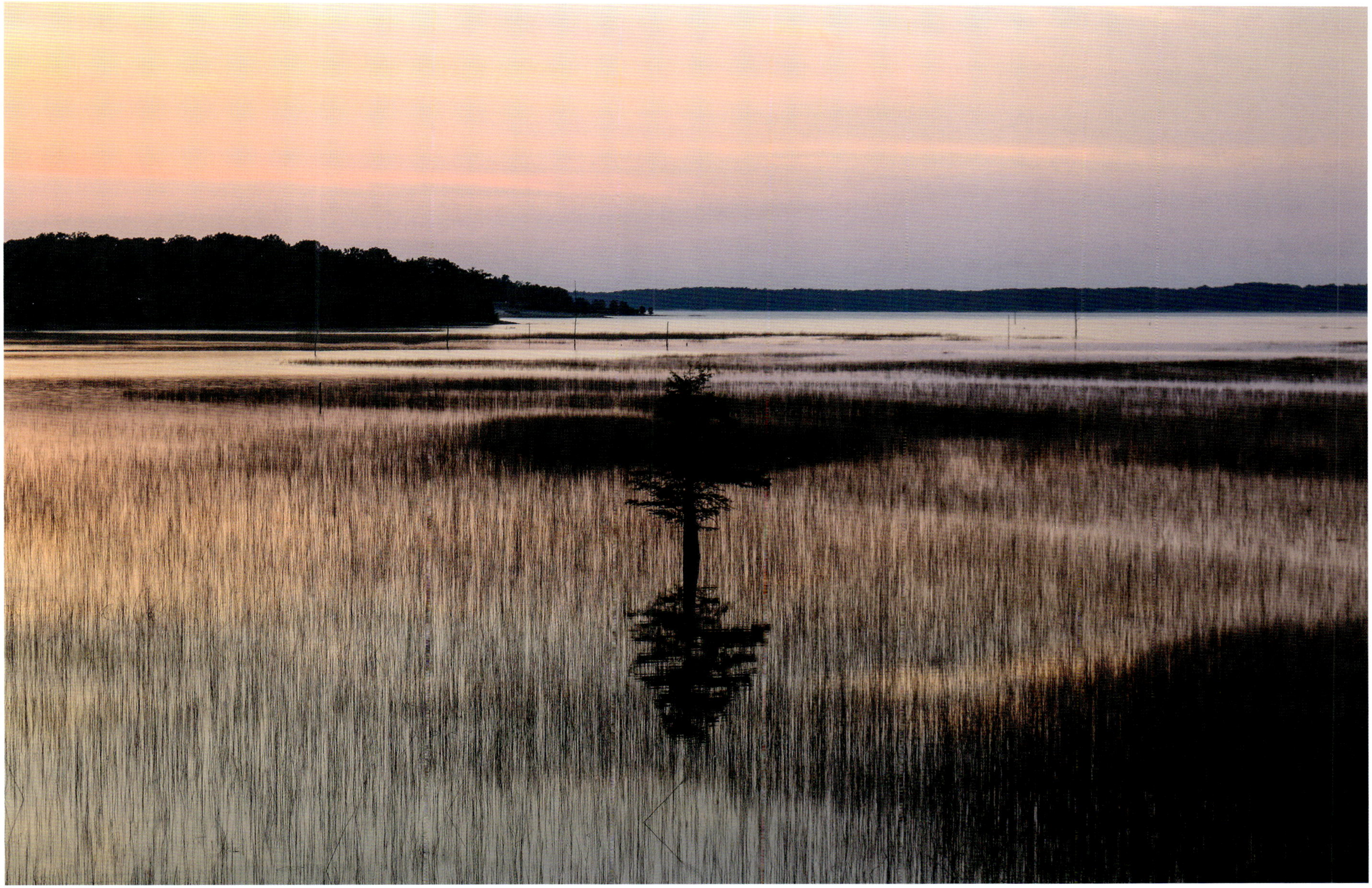

Why do you think you must have something to say?

The clouds do not speak. The water spreads
nearly to infinity

with its ragged hem of dark trees, and those grasses
there in the corner of your vision, the wind

moves them or does not move them.
They stretch forward into the light.

Lake, trees, sky—
look, everything is breathing.

You could put your fingers through these clouds.
Piled high above the lake, they're wet air, silence—

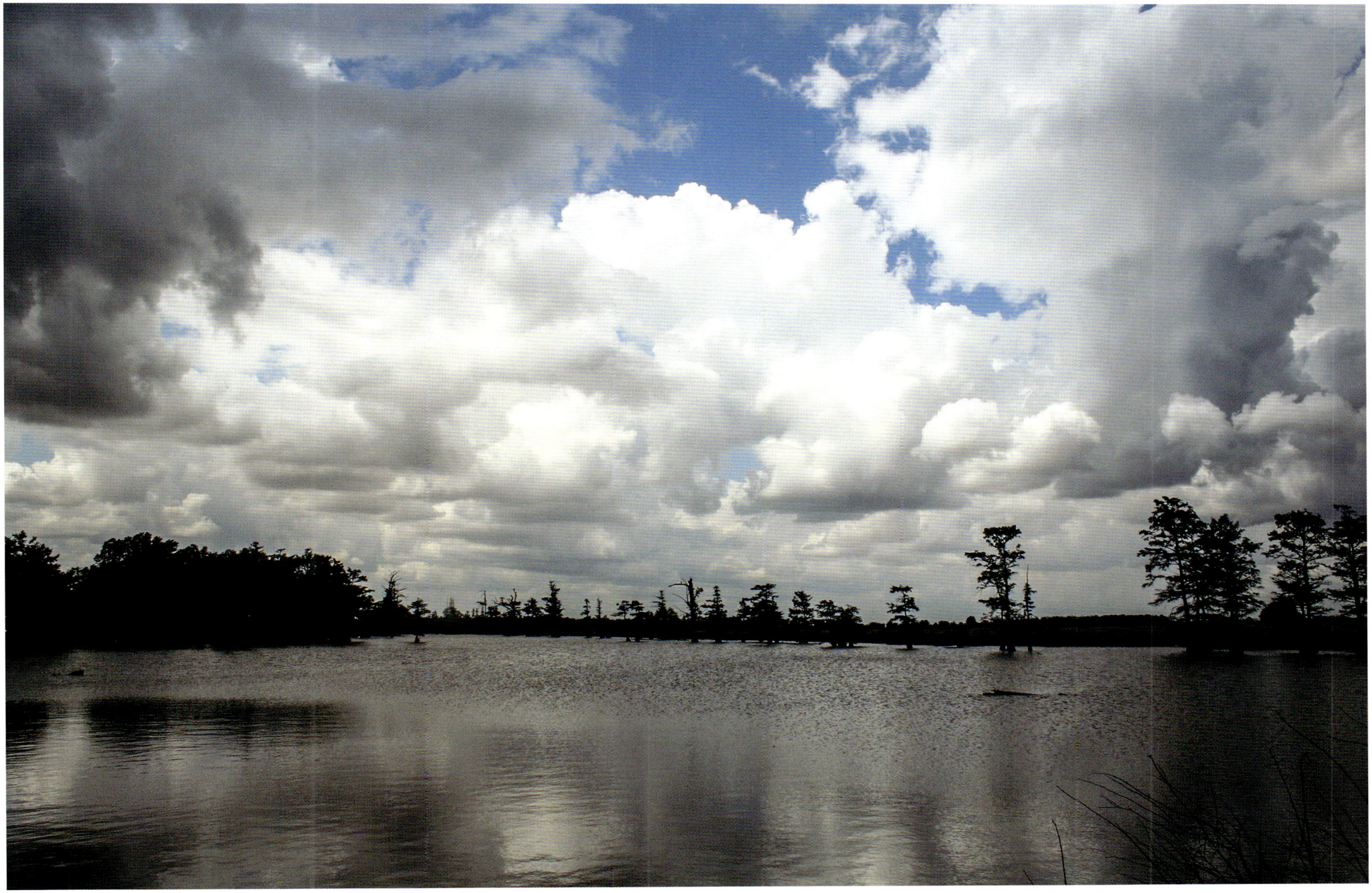

I wonder if the chair's still there

old wicker rocker my great aunt gave me
with a padded seat I had new covered

and pretty scrolls on the arms
white paint flaking but it rocked so good

for a while when it started to fall apart
I just used string tied it back together

one day passing he saw me
as I put it by the trash called *hey girl*
I'll take that off your hands
drag it to my porch in case someone wants to sit

he had a dog named Trixie
a Paul Scarlet rose plaster rabbits in the yard

that was such a time ago

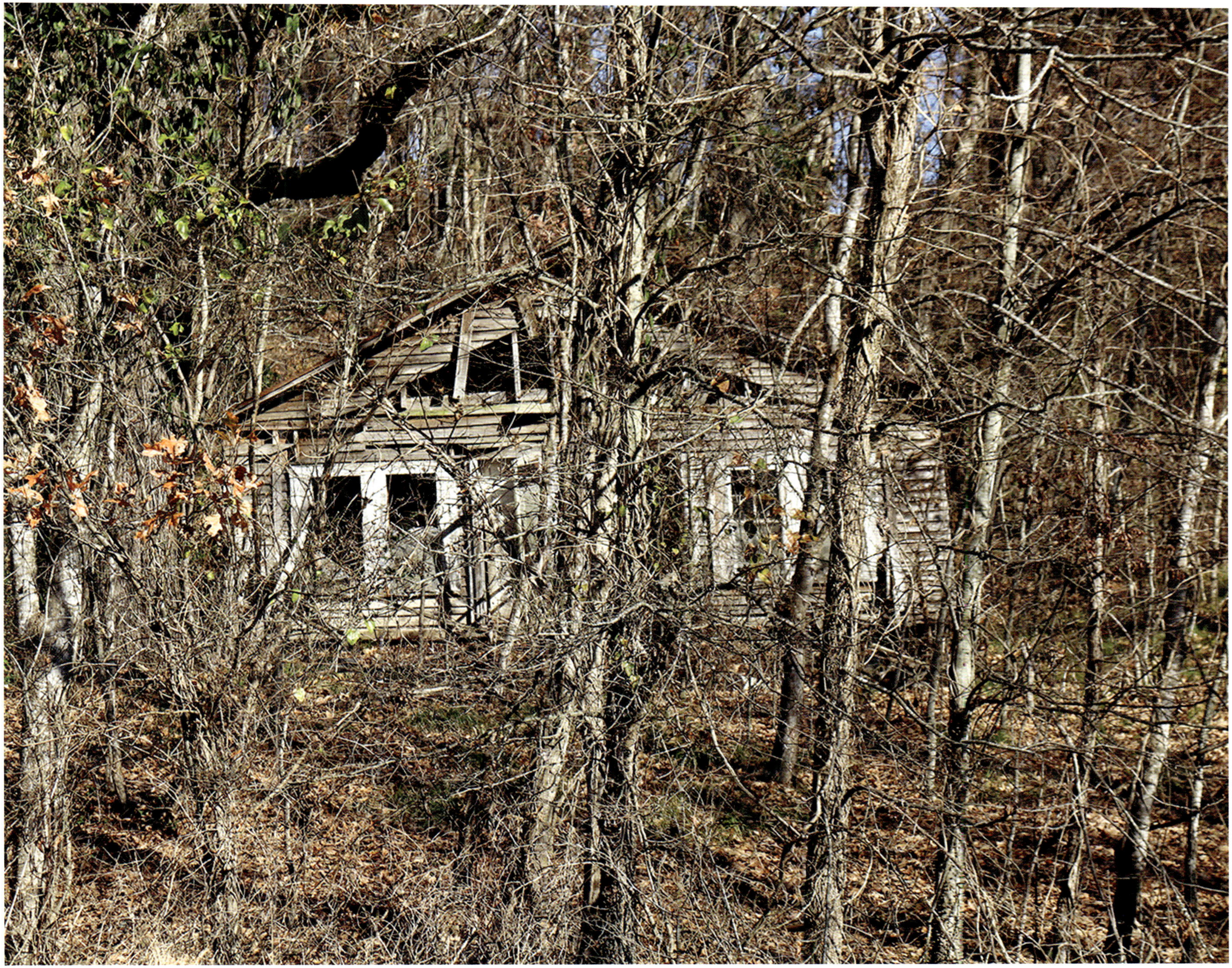

Once we drove to the lake
lay on his Chevy
to look at the stars
funny thing was no stars

but I could feel his heart
and hear the peepers singing

eeeeeeee eeeeeeee eeeeeeee eeeeeeee eeeeeeee eeeeeeee

hours and hours we lay there
he covered me with his coat
when I got cold

Once I think I dozed not dozed something stranger
than dozed
opened my eyes again

peepers still singing his heart still thumping
clouds whipped around
tearing holes in the sky

and shining through

was the moon

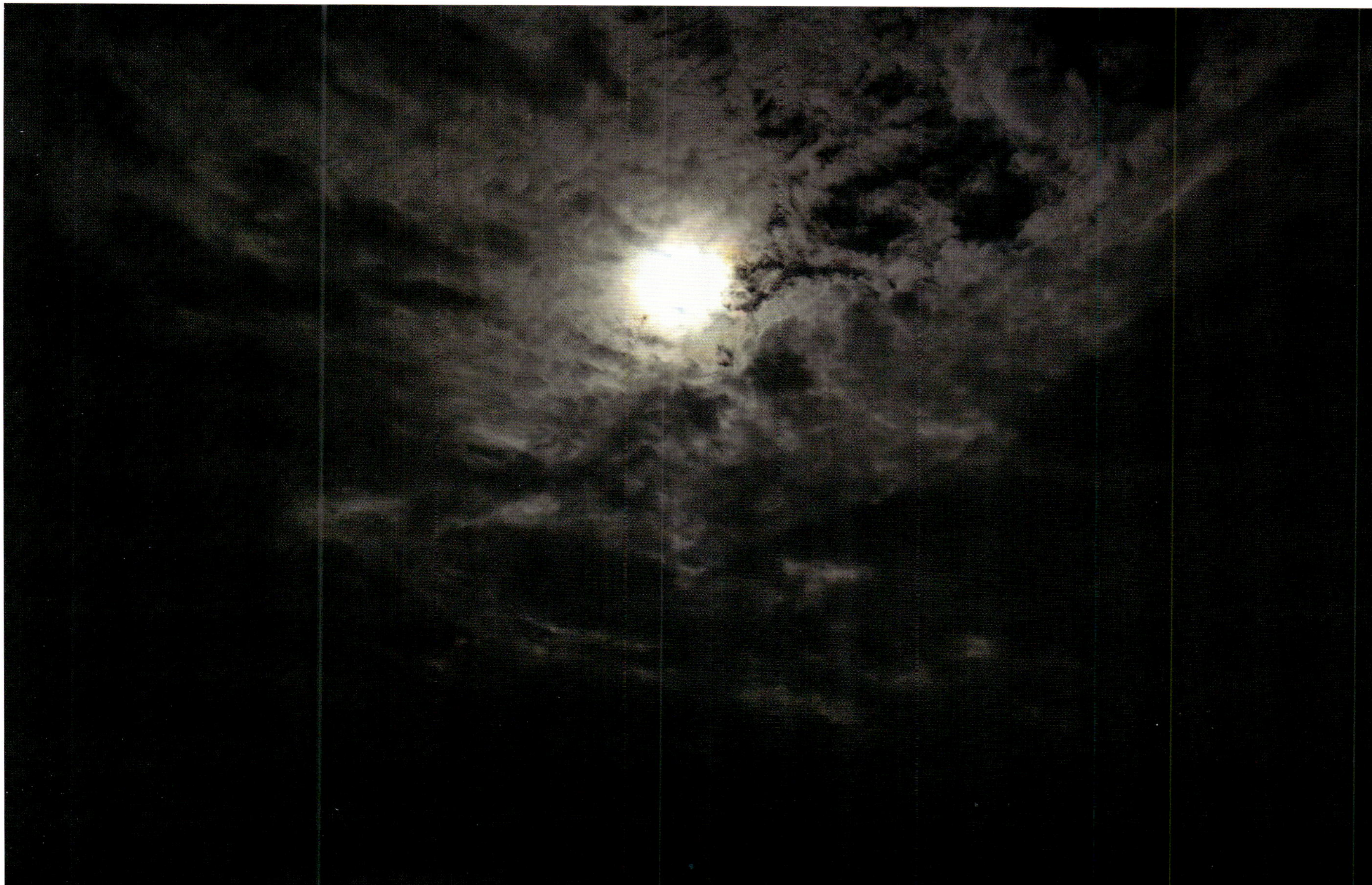

Just for a day as if it could
not be

I know what he done
and I ain't saying he shouldn't have to pay
but just for a day

as if it could
not be

pretty birds pretty birds
when I drove out to see him
snow geese speckle geese
flocking in the fields
like the Lord was shaking
salt and pepper
then rising to the skies
heading someway South

but the hard times follow

he be out soon
he be home soon

don't know what he going to do
don't know how he going to make it

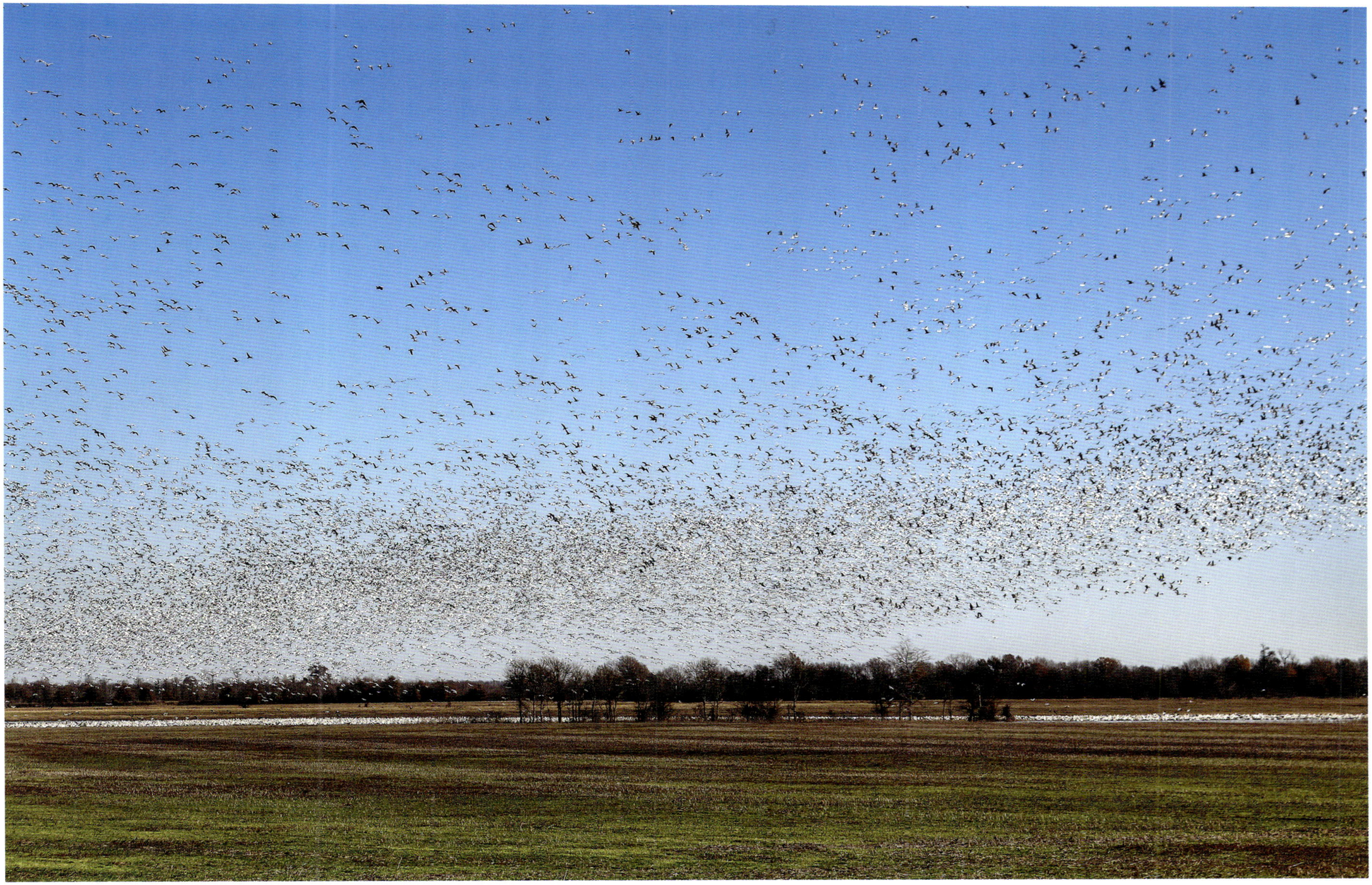

Well y'all knew Jimmy once he moved to Mississippi
but you didn't know him like I did
tiny little sprat with them jugears
runnin through the fields catchin crickets in a jar
or snugglin in bed
with this hairy stuffed rabbit he called Mr. Graysum

Mama and daddy didn't have much
first grade education sixth grade education
but what they had they gave us
good food grown in the fields
the strap when we was wicked
the habit of work   and love

Words don't go far to make you know the dead
I was his big brother

He built his house when he was young
chose every nail and drove it straight
and when he got it built he saw a little redhead
and determined he would marry her
Jimmy and Lorrie praise God amen
was married in peace for nearly 28 years

After she passed he couldn't abide the home fields
so he had to leave that life come down from Tennessee
and take shelter where we was

Four children twelve grandbabies all of them here today
drove day and night to get here
from Texas   Oklahoma   one his daughter Melanie
from her place outside Spokane
one his grandson Taylor from up by Butte Montana

Toward the end there wasn't nothin no medicine could do
this strong man saved in Jesus
went walkin through the shadow and the valley

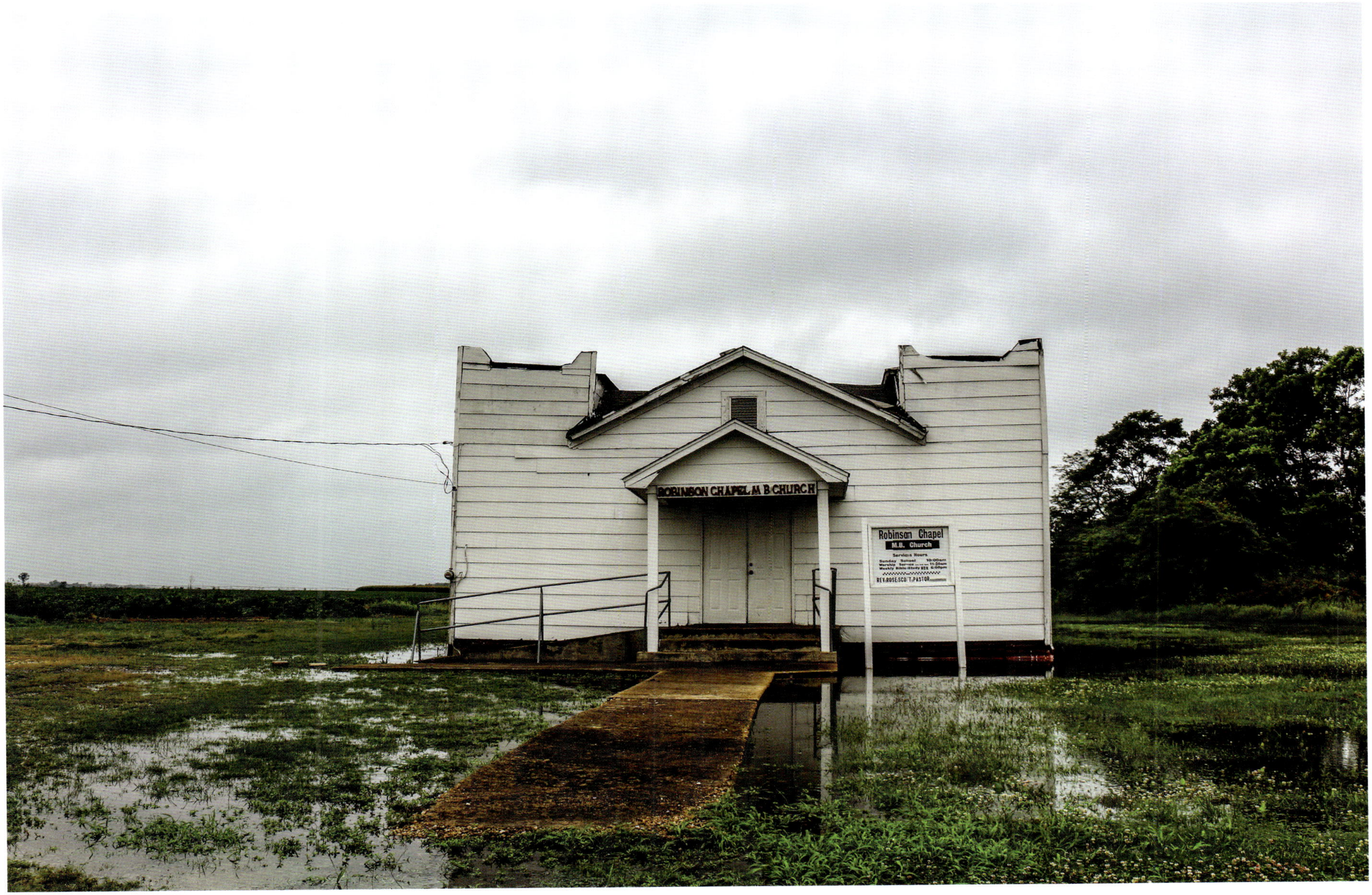
ROBINSON CHAPEL M B CHURCH
Robinson Chapel
M.B. Church
Sunday School 10:00am

I do not like snake   he be mean
        he hang from the trees
                and get in your boat
or sometime he swim through the water

and more than snake be trouble
        some say the dead
                        hang round here
reach up through the water
                                drag you down

        after that boy got shot
                I heard him
                        in among the skeeters
and the peepers   moanin for mercy

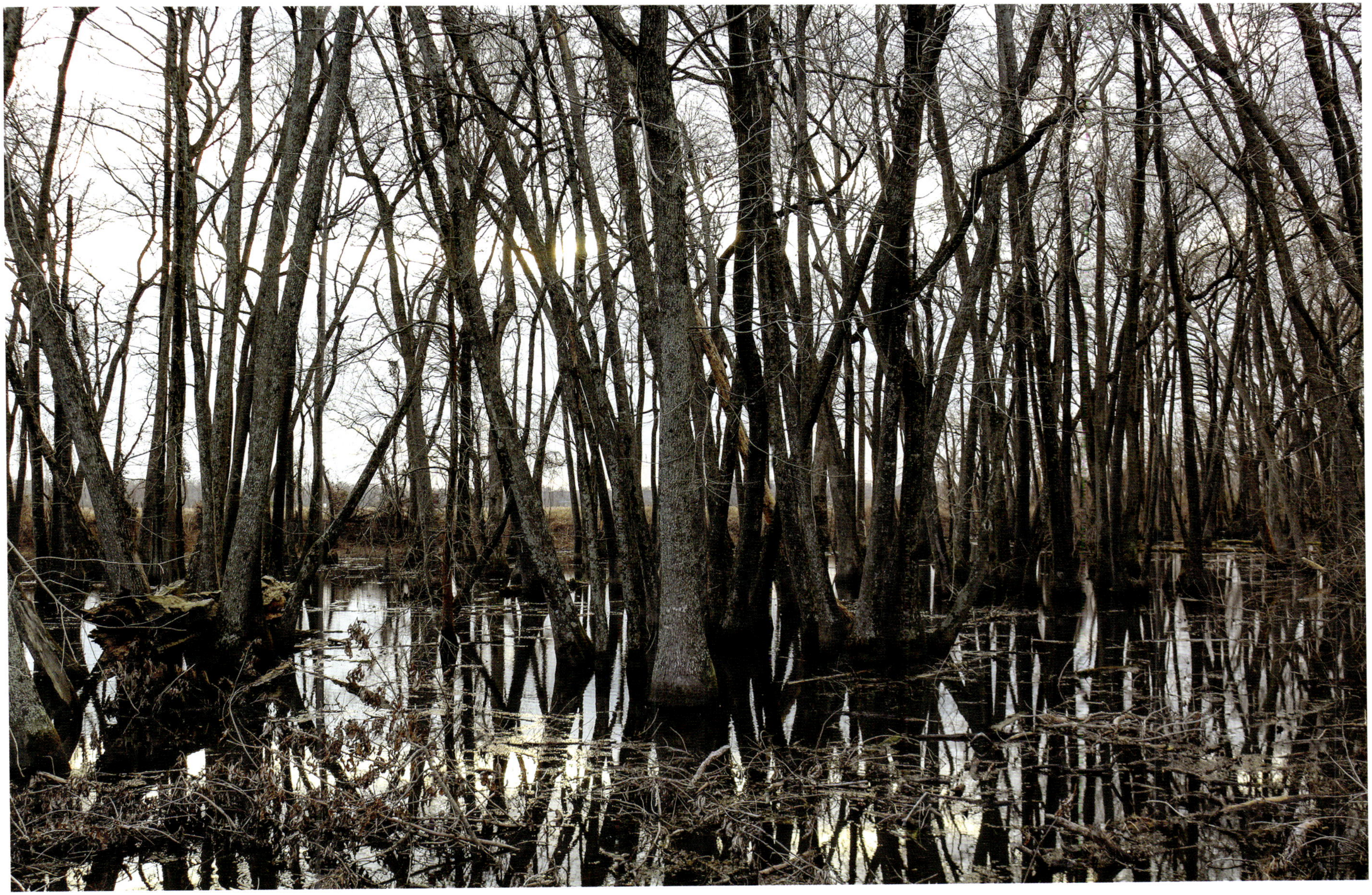

When it commenced it come on fast
and she wouldn't let nobody touch her
just kept whispering

Lordhavemercylordhavemercylordhavemercy

up and down
up and down breathing in and out till it
all run together like a river

all night all day she worked on birthing that baby
wasn't nothing they could do
even her mamma and the midwife

at the end I went outside I damned God I said
Do it to me too just do it

fell to my knees beneath that final light

buried them in a single coffin
in among the trees

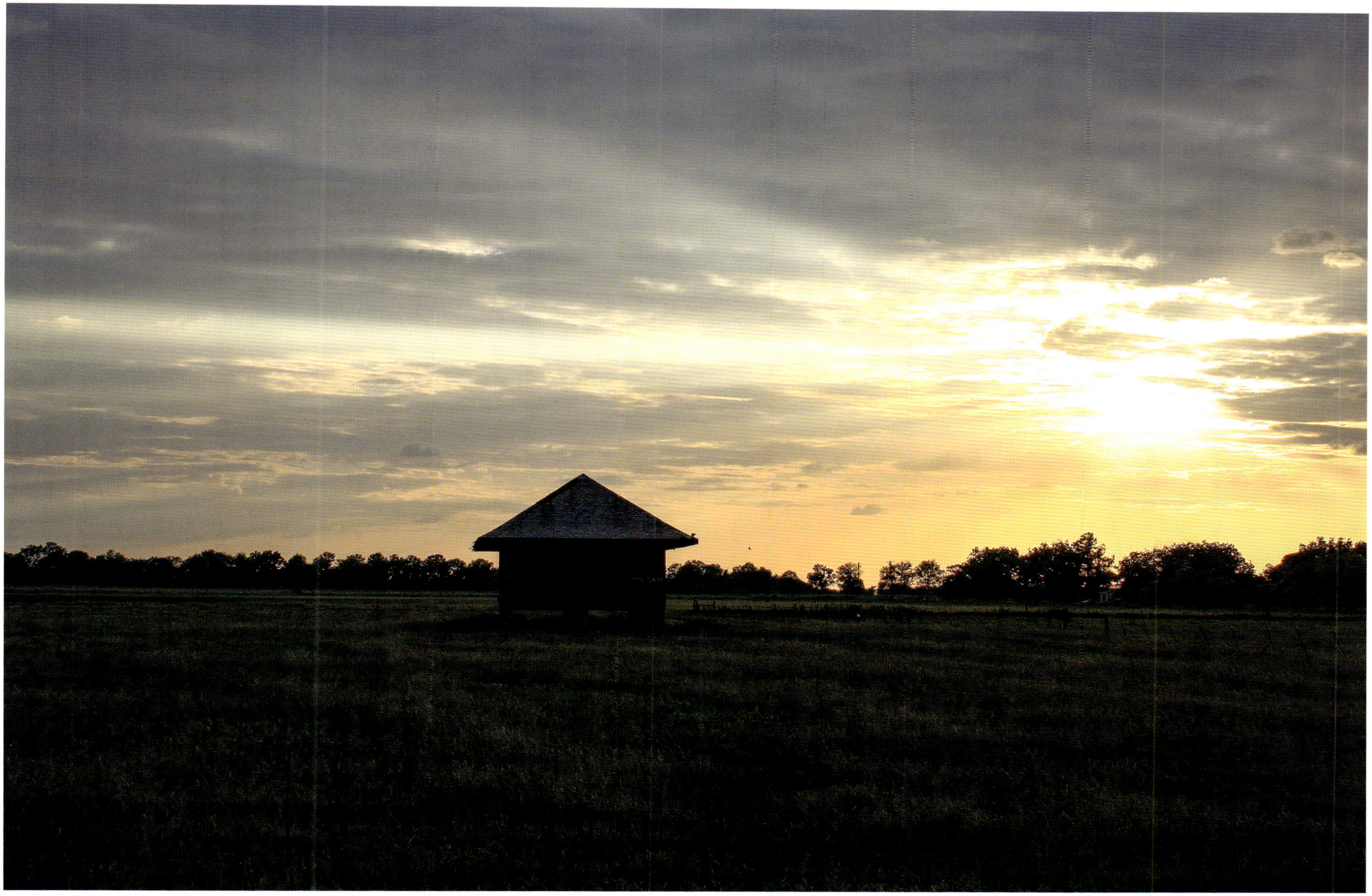

Go ahead you stinkin
bag of filth
clean up that field
pick them slick squirrel
guts clean leave only
that matted fur to get
rained on stomped into
the weeds till there is
no more squirrel when
you lift off and roost
in the trees you so
heavy you shake
the branches go ahead
turkey buzzard make
my day swoop on down
swayin like a rockin
chair there's nothin
around here anymore
anyway since the plant
closed since the kid died
I know you're watchin
me think I'm next in line
huh just do your job
and eat it up
the glistenin headless

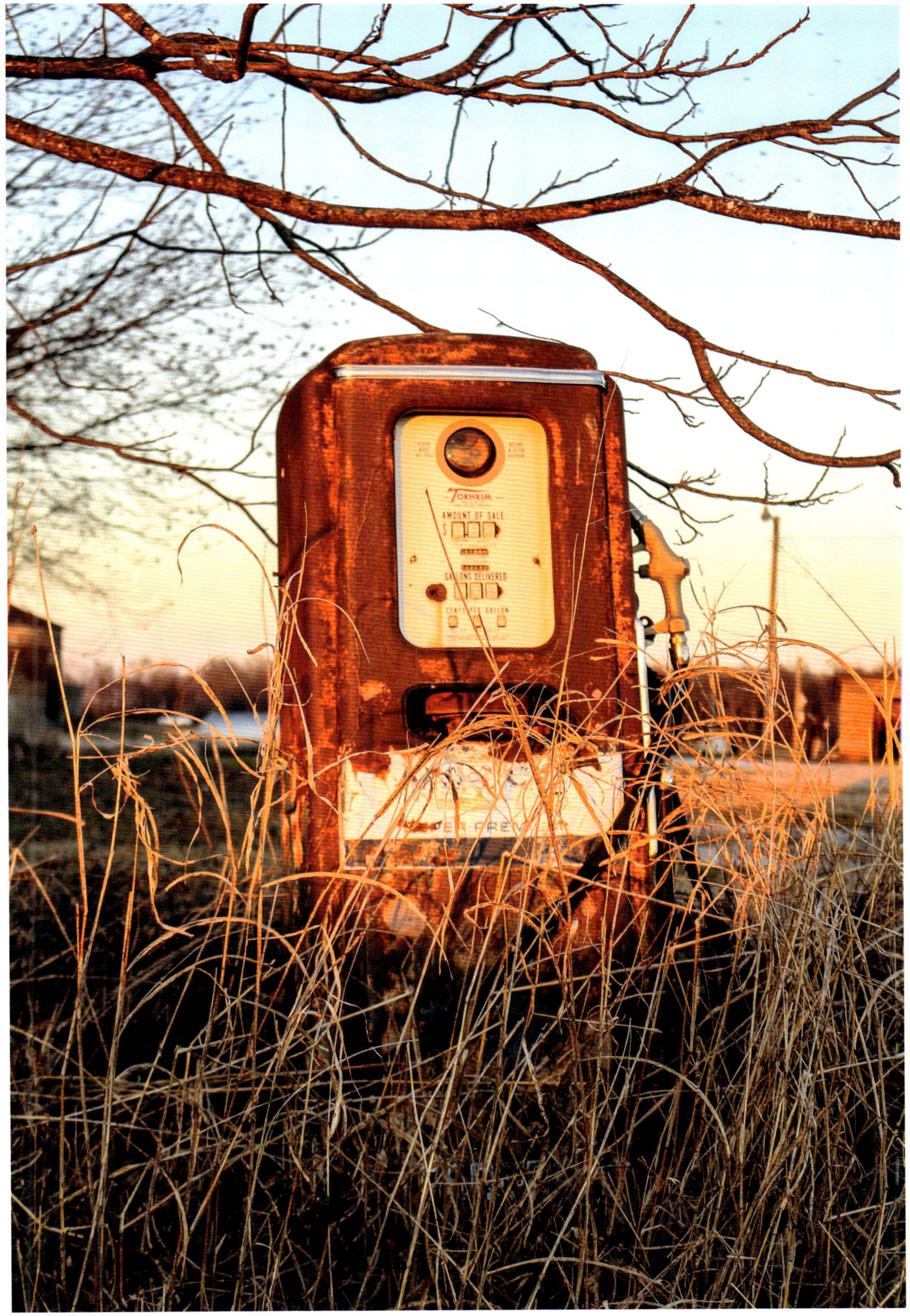
AMOUNT OF SALE
GALLONS DELIVERED
CENTS PER GALLON

Devil each night he come around my door
devil each night he linger by my door
call me like the hoot owl
Hoo hoo
real soft like in the woods
wisht I couldn't hear him no more

I can't shake that devil
got to shake that devil and ride
can't shake that devil
got to shake that devil and ride
wake up in the darkness
devil right by my side

My body bound for glory
but my soul she clinging here below
body bound for glory
but my soul she clinging here below
know Jesus love my body
but the devil sure damn my soul

Gonna put my pants and shoes on
set off down that midnight road
put my pants and broken shoes on
set off down that road
when the fires light up the morning
gonna lay down this load

Devil he put the stars out
take away the moon
devil he put the stars out
take away the moon
since I took to wickedness
devil gonna take me soon

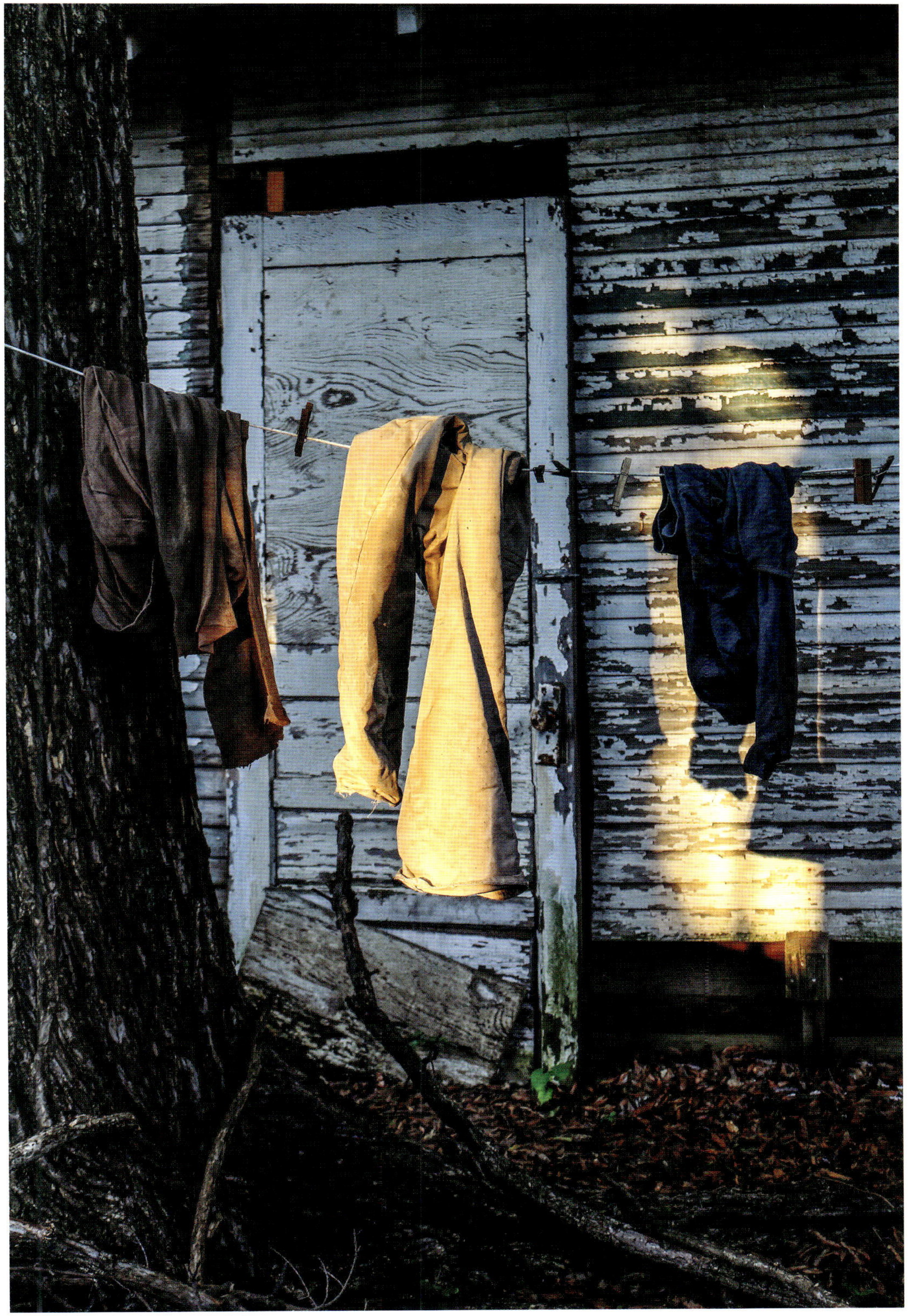

He ain't done right to whistle
and talk *hi y'all baby* and filth
to Carolyn Bryant even if he come

from away he ought to known
how we do around here and I sure
as hell don't believe his uncle

shoulda stood up and pointed out
Roy and J.W. in that courthouse
I am so blessed tired of people

students and all coming down here
to interview us just because we
was alive then making out like this

is a bad town y'all don't know
what we do for those who know
their place why just yesterday

Polly I said to the woman who
takes care of me *my husband don't*
use this red tee and these shoes

take em for Brewster as for the rest
why that was a long time ago
most folks dead and store collapsed
to ruins why you raking it up again

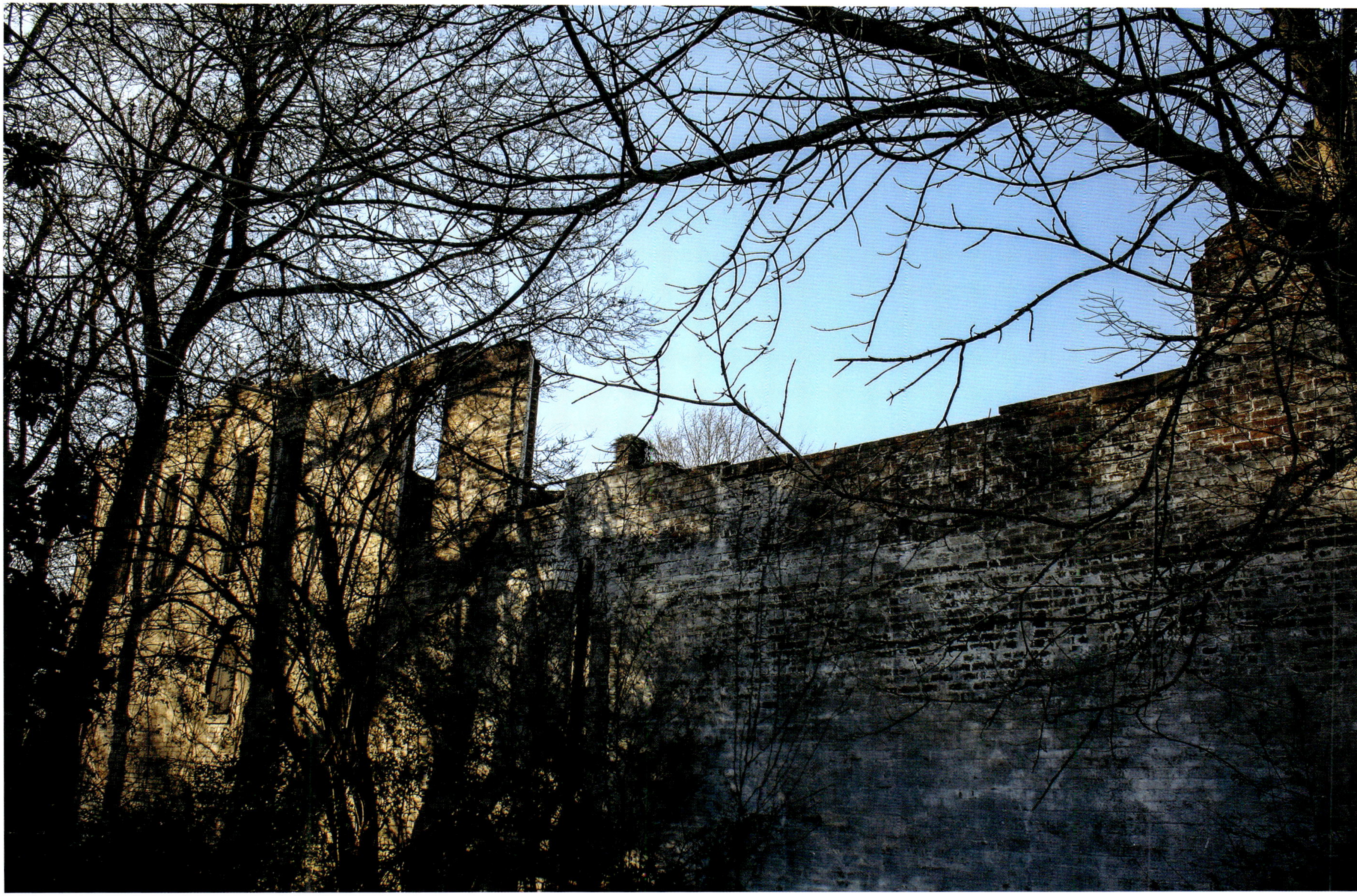

Well you know back then couldn't no
black man see justice
down here

so when Mr. Wright come out that door
after standing up in court and
pointing out the killers he

was marked for a dead man
had to hightail to the station
leave his cotton in the fields

and get on out of here
I was just a kid
didn't think like my folks

was ashamed what they be doing
so when they was talking that night
over chicken and collards

saying *get the sheets*
go rough up some a them teach em
what's right I snuck off

hid in my closet prayed *Pray Lord*
didn't have no words
for my misery just *Pray Lord*

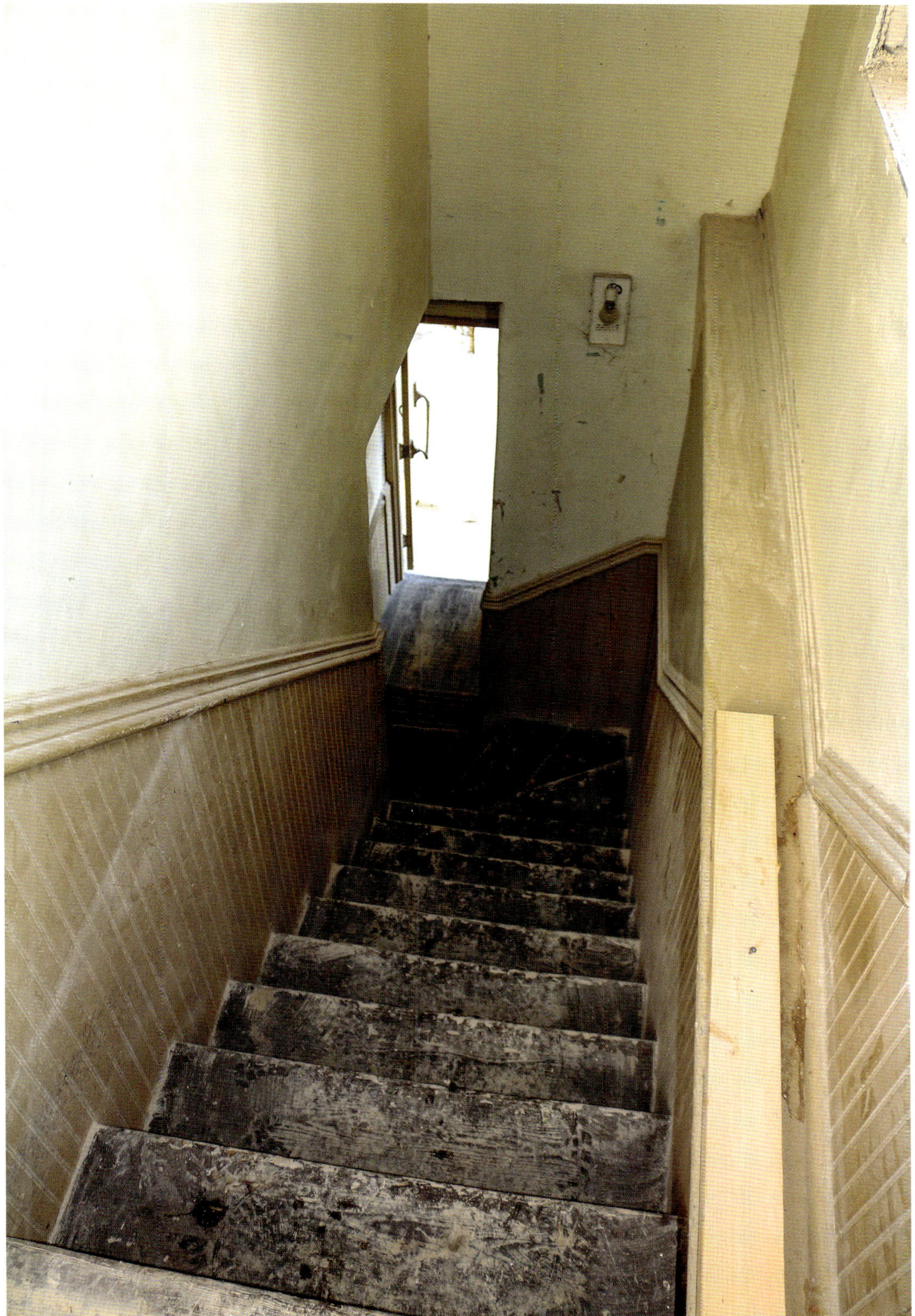

Yeah   man
skank ho left
and took the little tv   I was so pissed
I went out back where the dumpster
stinks of bones and rotten
b-b-cue and such
and shot the window
my own window   dumbass
nothing to do but tape it up
ha
see how it looks like the Flag
the way I taped that window

It don't make no sense
why she left
we had a good life   beer in the cooler
weed by the bed   party lights going
me reaming her good
then one day she
threw her shit in a suitcase
snatched up the tv
stormed out of here
I'll see you in hell
now it's closing in around me
not a night but I don't hear gunshot

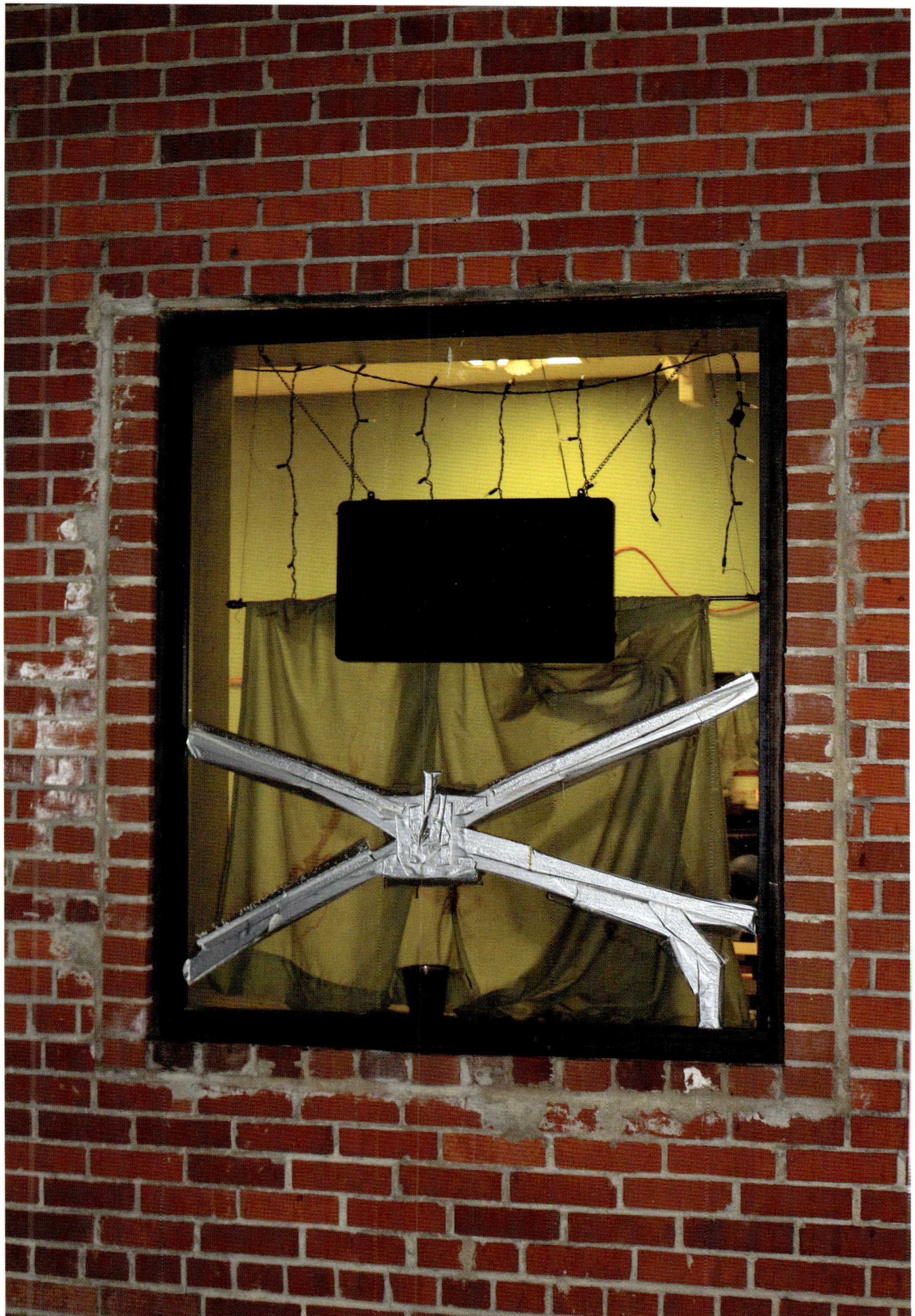

—*Take that flag down*,
says the old inmate whose name
I don't know, who sits across from me

in the circle in the Parchman
Prison classroom where I've come
with Patrick and Otis, my colleagues

who teach the history of civil rights,
where they talk and I listen
about Fannie Lou Hamer, about

the Mississippi Freedom
Democratic Party and *I'm sick*
and tired of being sick and tired,

and where Otis, who's white and comes
from Charleston, struggles not to weep
as he talks about the last few days

in Charleston. *Take that flag down*,
the old man repeats, *still won't nothing*
change. Flag ain't nothing but a bandaid.

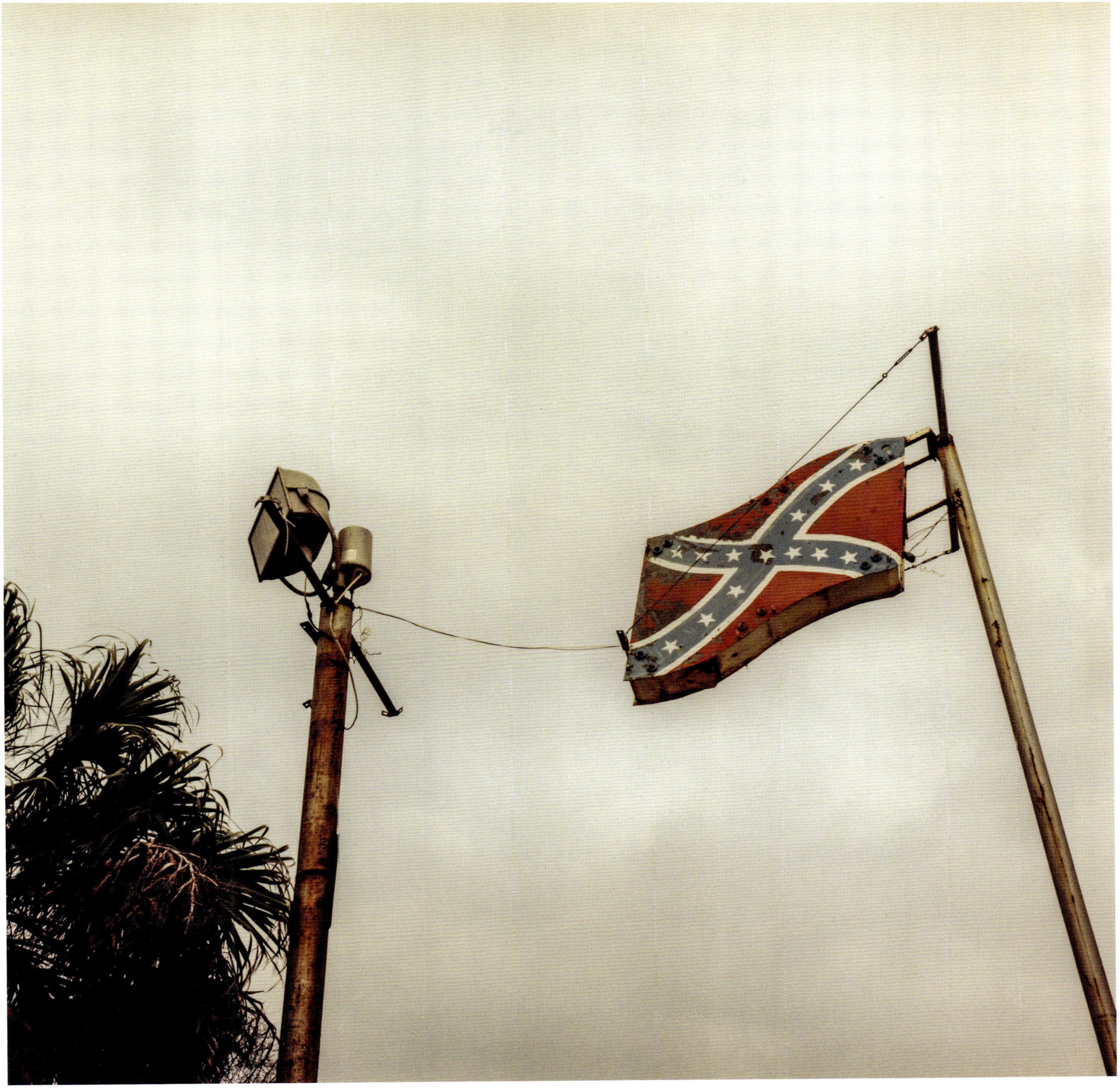

I'm scared, if I get senile
like my mama,
I'll start thinking, like she did,
that every black man is out to rob me.
Scared I'll start blurting the words
that sometimes throng my brain,
words I grew up with
along with croquet in the summer,
crystal swans and silver salvers—
nigra, nappyhead, step aside boy
…and worse. Dear God, purify my heart.
Or if you can't do that, seal my lips.

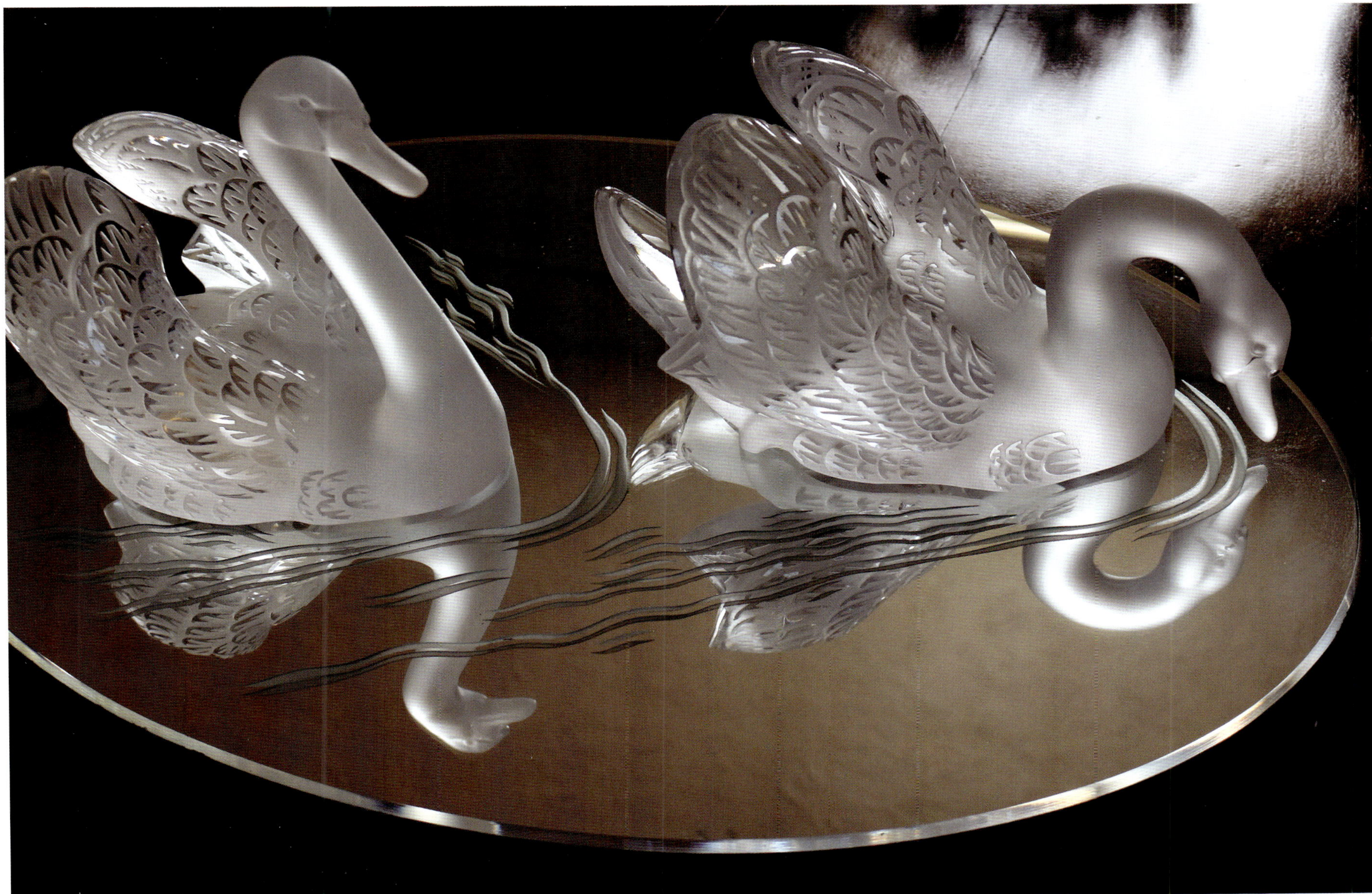

Thirty-five years
        we've lived in Mississippi

                Today listening
            to the radio
my husband tells me
        Dylan's 75 today

                First time I heard him
            Baez pulled his
scrawny ass on stage
        to sing *Blowin' in*
                the Wind maybe
            Hattie Carroll
at the Berkeley
        Folk Music Festival
                where Lightnin'
            Hopkins dragged
a straightback
        wooden chair
                to a single mike
            and in that summer

of snarling dogs
        on the end of chains
                and fire hoses that I'd
            watch every night
on TV and vow
        never never never
                to live in the South
            Hopkins sang
I'm gonna walk with
        the Prince of Peace
                down by the riverside
            down by the riverside

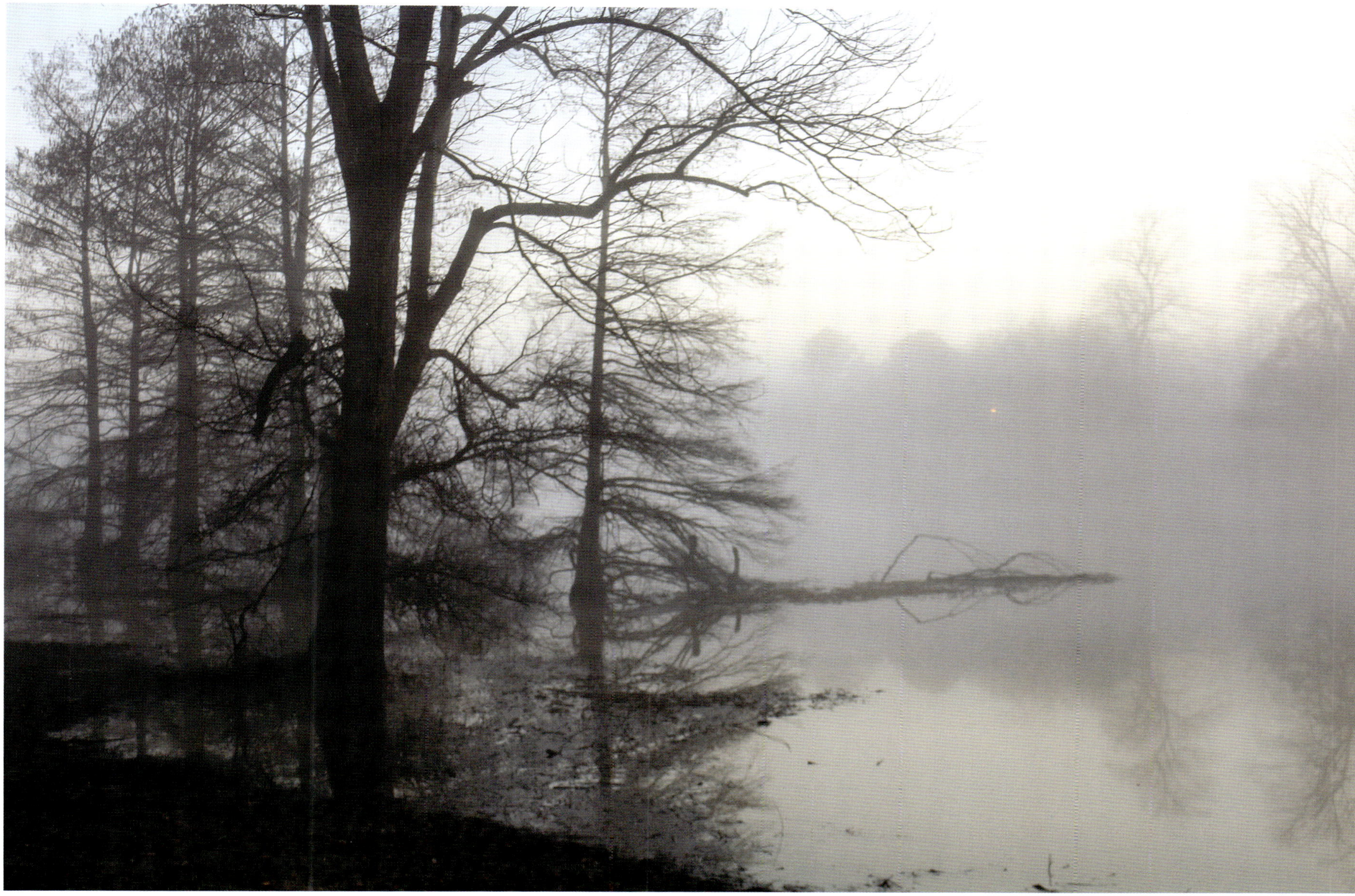

He's waiting at the crossroads
dressed in a long black coat
and crimson shoes in his left hand
he carries a willow wand waving it
he says *Come forward* and you do

you are hesitant and shy
yet full of singing
beyond you the river shines
the river that swallows the radiant boatmen

Why do you wonder
if this is Mr. Death
because that is what the song says
that only death could offer such transformation?

in his pocket sprigs of lilac and thyme
sheltered in the crook of his right arm
something you do not see it is dark
with feathers a hen an owl a mockingbird

he waits for you say yes
beyond him the water is silver and silver
but how can there be a crossroads
where there is water?
which of the roads leads endlessly into the river?

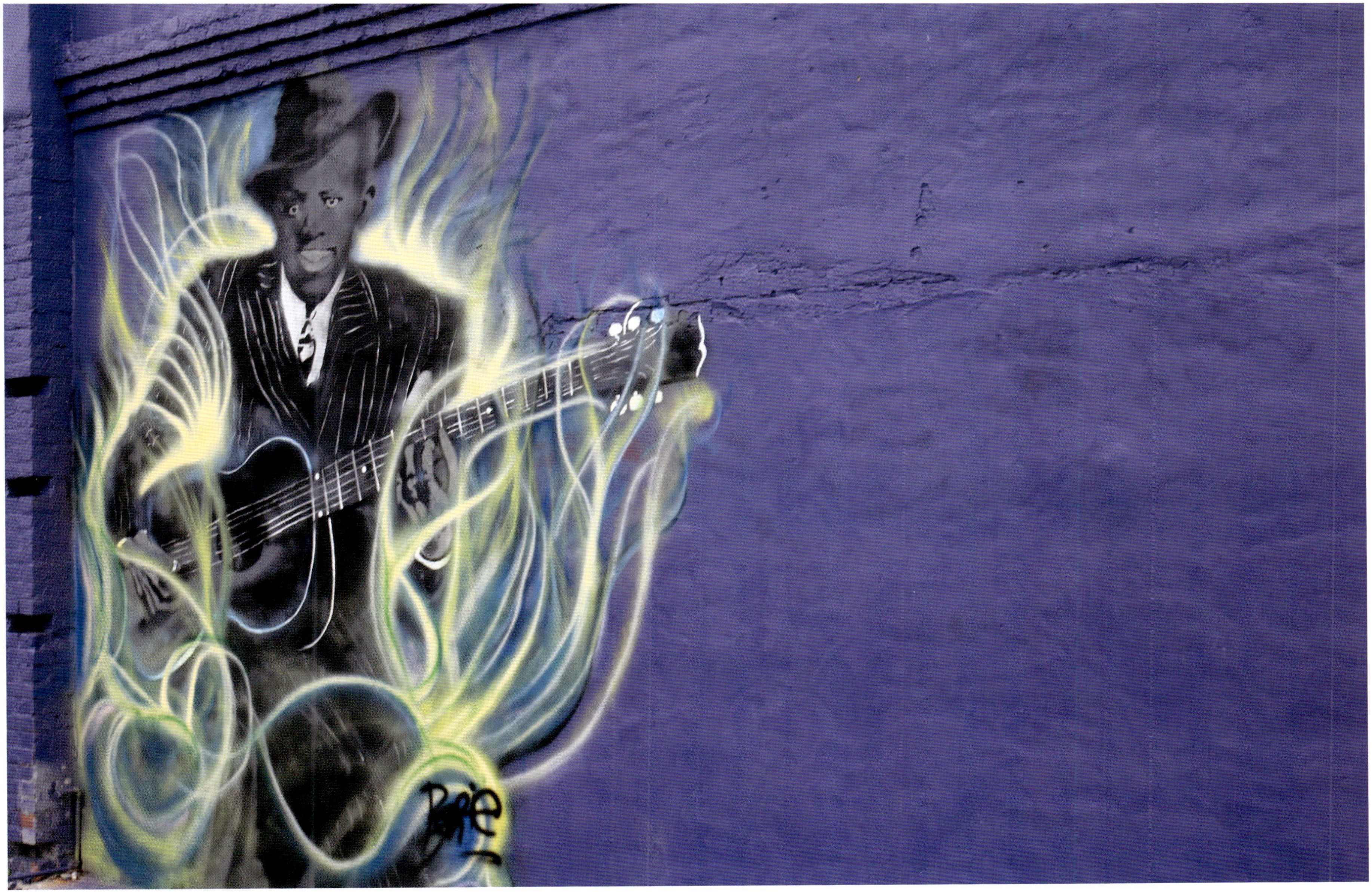

We was walking home from prom
I was kicking the petals

when he pulls out this ring

says he bought it
for another girl
Lorraine

but when he saw me at the game
he changed his mind

I don't care
never had much

folks say I'm pretty
but shy as the back of the moon

I love that little dimple he has
love him
and I'm going to marry him

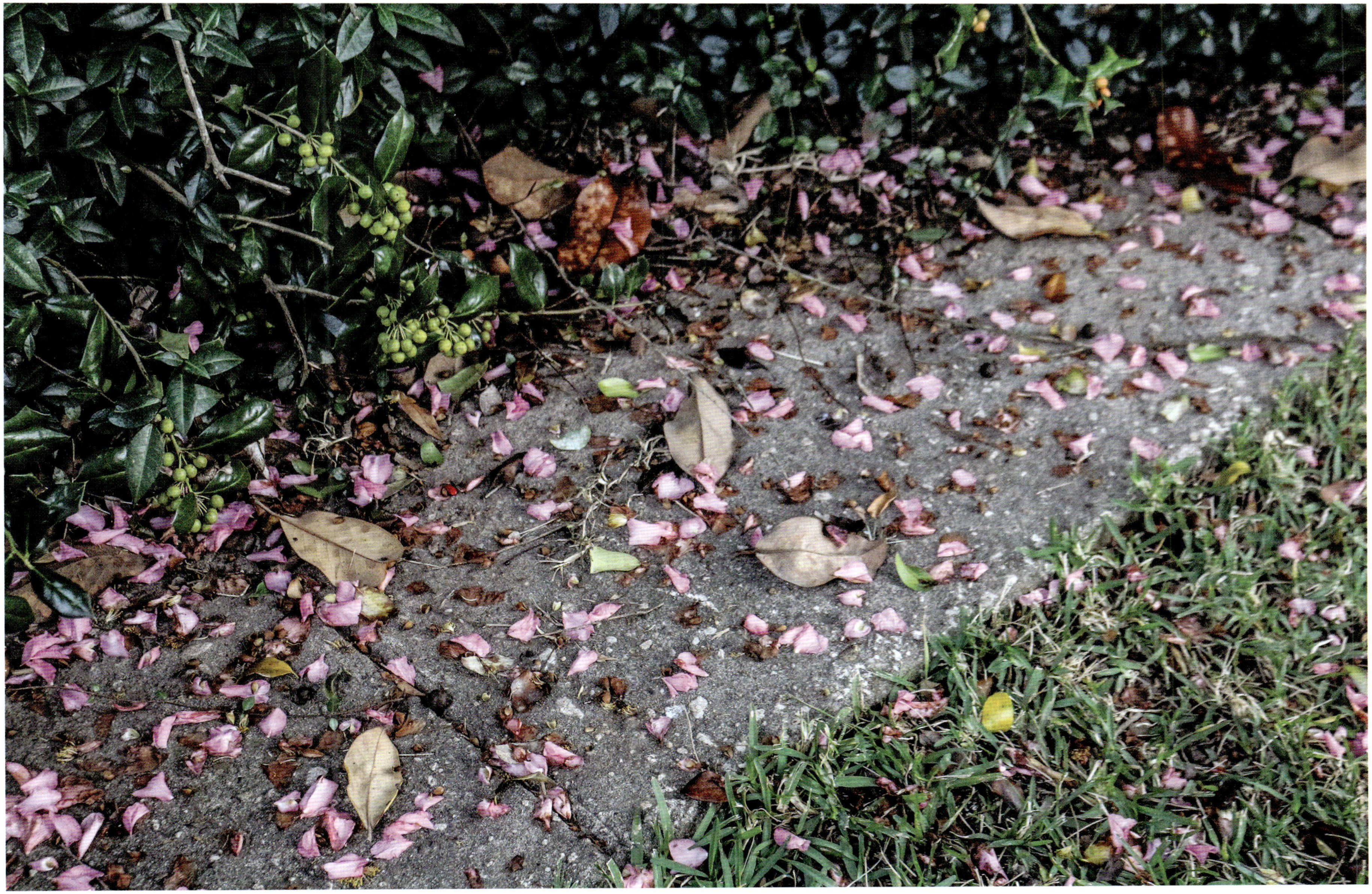

I'd never stayed in such a place—
like a castle, all lit up and gleaming,
looming out of the dark as we were driving
toward the mountains. But he said yes,
we could. So we got a room, filled a bath,
climbed in the clawfoot tub, lay back
legs all tangled, and ate strawberries,
strawberries, strawberries we'd picked
in a muddy Pic-Your-Own field just when
the rain stopped, toward twilight. Berries
so ripe we couldn't eat them fast enough.
That hotel was kind to us— anonymous
and secret, with deep woven rugs
that caught the moonlight, and later
the high white bed. Toward midnight,
unable to sleep, we went out into
hilly streets that led through darkness.
Sister Laurent once read to us,
What thou lovest well remains. I wanted
to remain, though I knew our lives
led back to the city, back to pain.
So I willed our shades to stay there.
And I said to him, *There they go.*
They will walk forever down the streets
of Balsam Gap. We will not see them again.

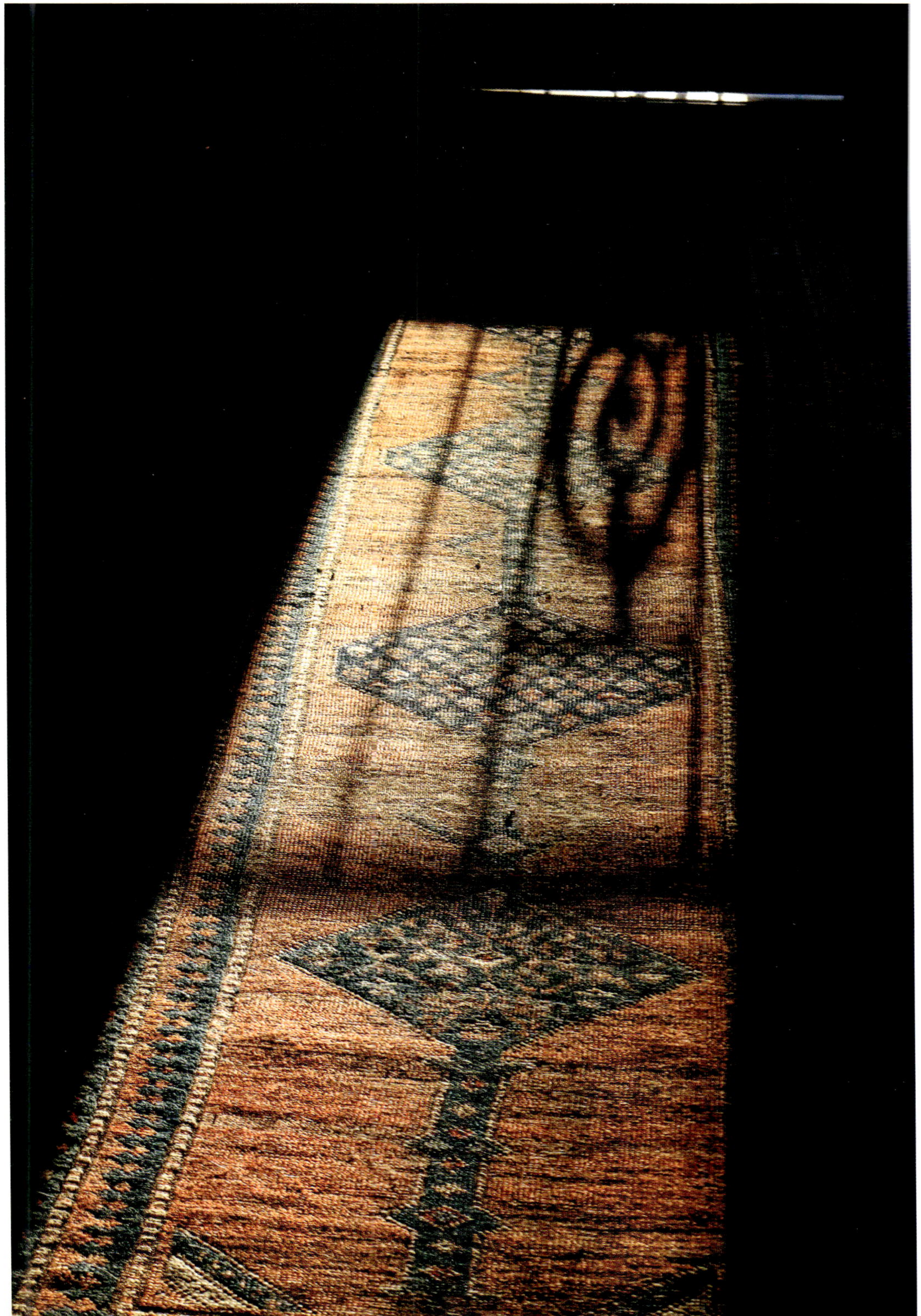

Your hands on my face

your belly   on my belly

me flipping like a fish at the bottom of a boat
nip   *nip*   sharp nails
your butt your back

don't want to hurt you honey
want to tear you down to the bone

afterwards   washing   peeing

looselimbed back to bed
to the valleys and the shadows
and a redbird at the window

wearing your old blue robe
you bring me fruit in a silver cup

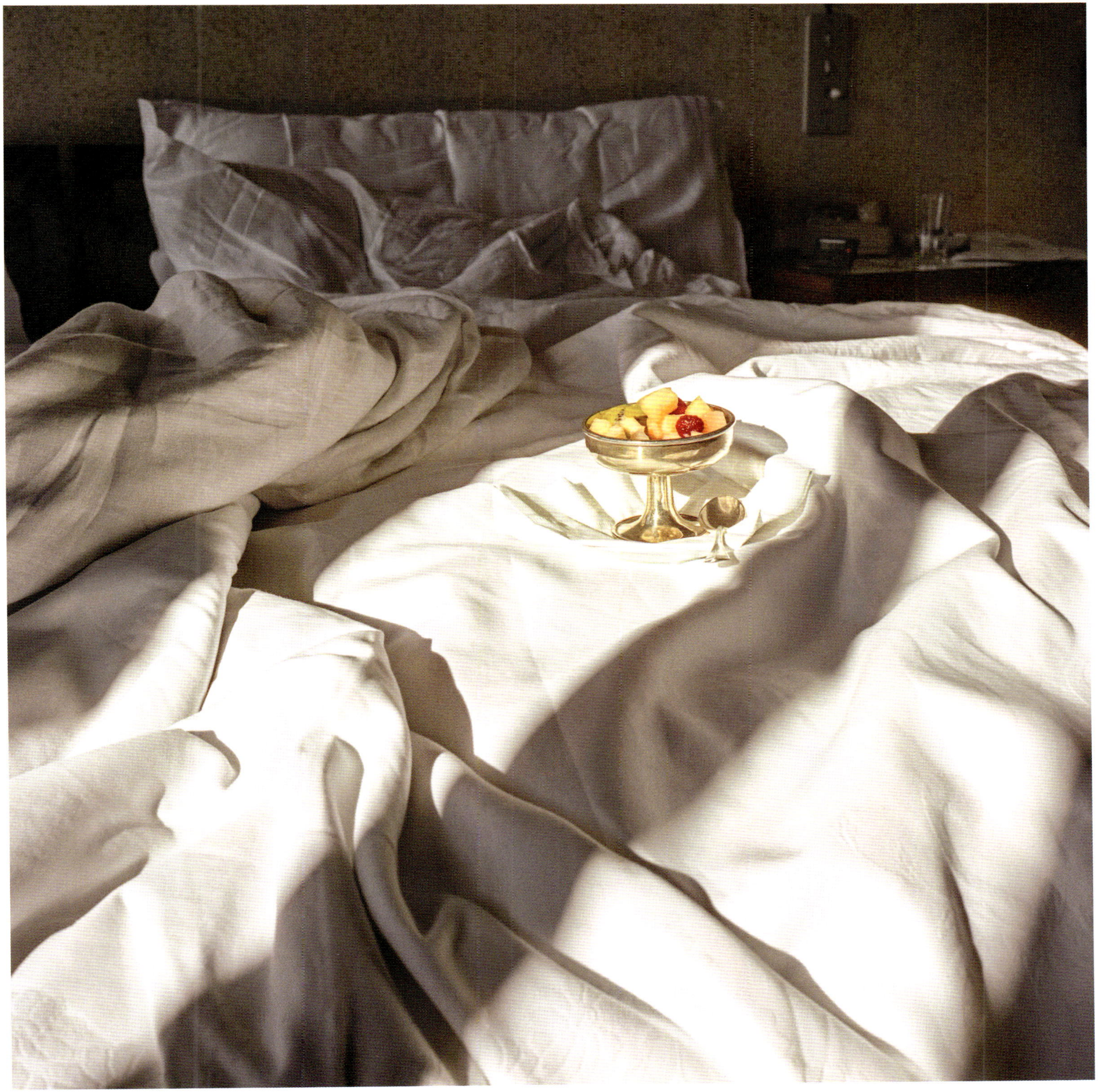

I saw the most beautiful boy today
jogging across campus
lifting his knees high
proud pony
hair that rippled to his shoulders
pulled through a backwards baseball cap

He didn't appear to labor
didn't glance to either side

Oh I think I am just a cliché
to them all
poor thing, they say, with that face
and so old-fashioned

Sometimes as I teach
I find I'm playing with my bracelet
every tiny charm
something my father brought me
from his stations in the Army
a fan, the Eiffel tower
a ballerina *en pointe*
a cuckoo as from a cuckoo clock
three gold hearts, a cluster of bells
and my favorite, from Japan, an ivory gardenia

I saw the most beautiful boy

and I wanted to lay him down
run my fingers along his cheek
linger at the hyoid bone
trace the sternum and rippling ribs
stop at the elegant iliac crest

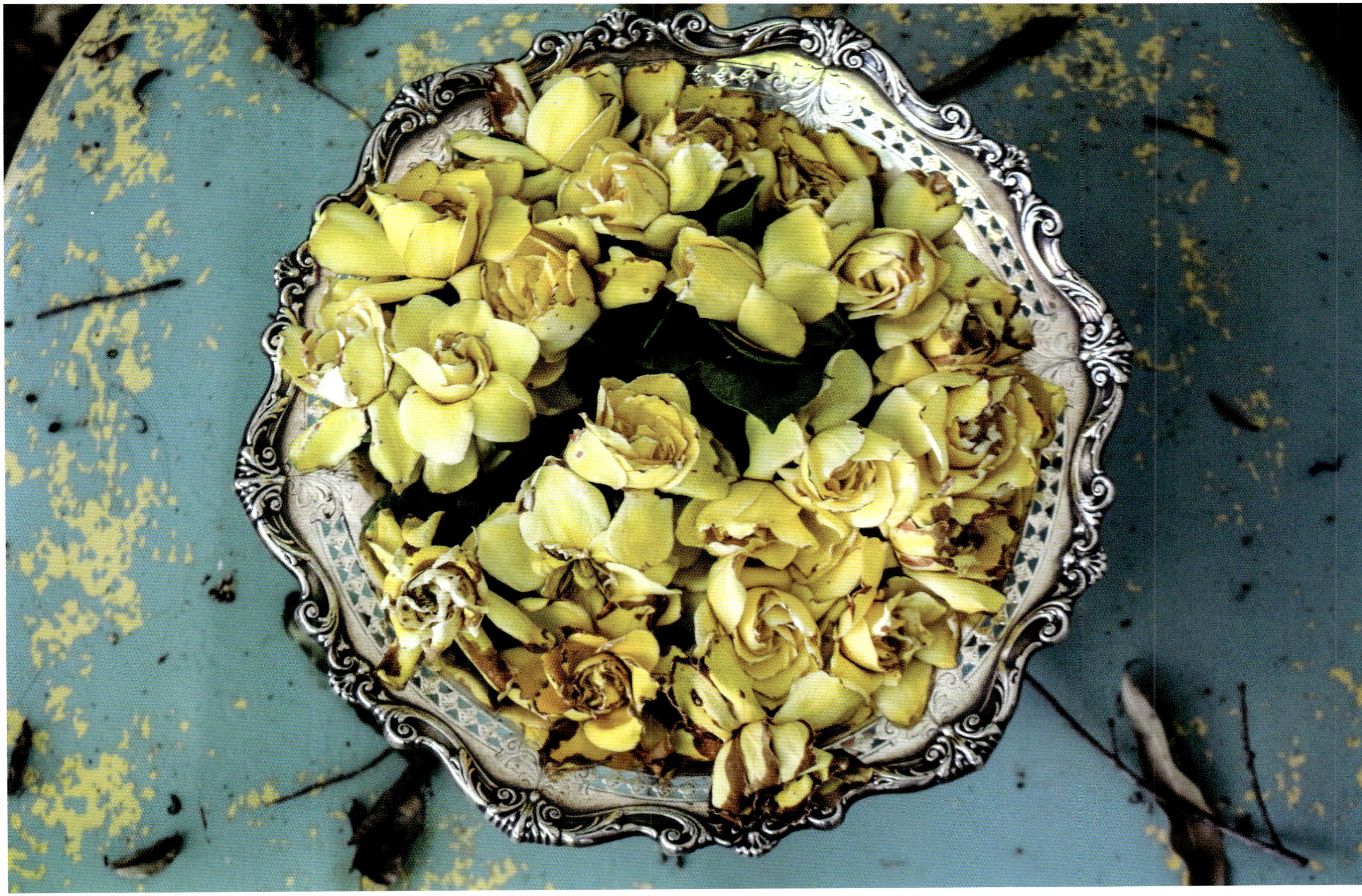

Like to drove me crazy
the cicadas in the privet and pecan trees
whupping up their little motors
all those nights

like beating the eggs for angel cake
I'd churn that eggbeater
faster and faster
till my hand got tired let it fall back quiet

then oh shoot eggwhites not stiff enough
so here we go again

and them crickets
chirping and buzzing all silvery and tinkly
summer nights as I laid by Bobby

one day he flipped his ATV
hurt his foot couldn't drive no longer
so we retired
bought a cabin out by Sardis

but we were happy in that house
fan stirring   sheets damp
he'd lick the salt right off my neck

all those bugs clamoring up
like love

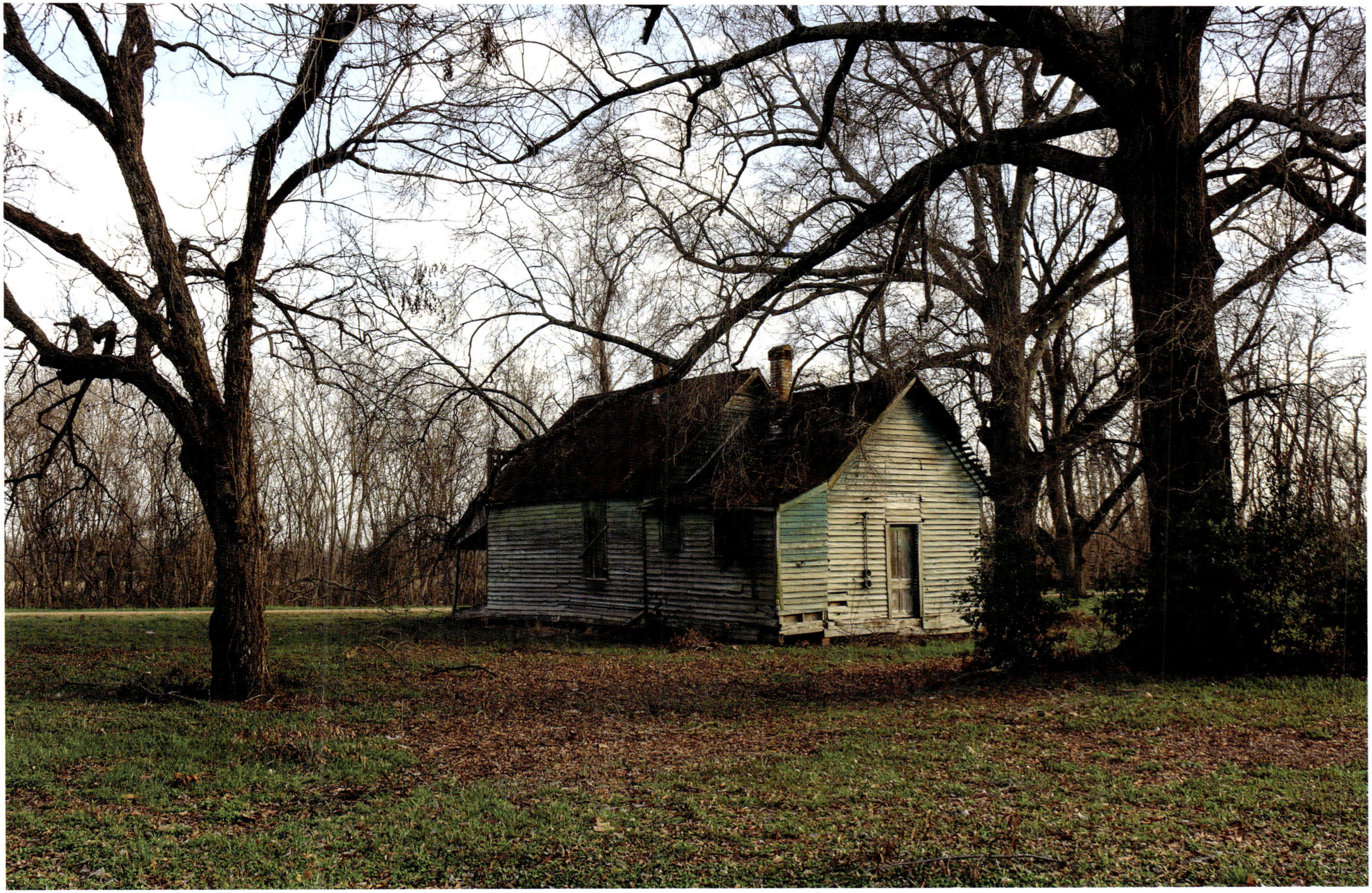

When daddy died mamma said *you are too young to wear black*
    your navy blue dress will do nicely

high-necked collar   woolen   drab
        double-breasted with gold buttons
                                I remember
this terrible silence
                we stood in the rain and Mr. Paxton
said the 23rd Psalm   all that fall
        it never ceased to rain   nobody cried
that wasn't our way nobody even touched or hugged

    mamma moved around the house
a silent   numb Calvinist   wraith

but when Trey laid me down and started scrabbling at my tights
    in the back of his car
        I pushed him away

            I started sobbing I saw daddy
    like this light
beyond the shadows that were our bodies

through that domed metal roof   through the pine trees
    through the rain
        close as my heartbeat   looking down at me

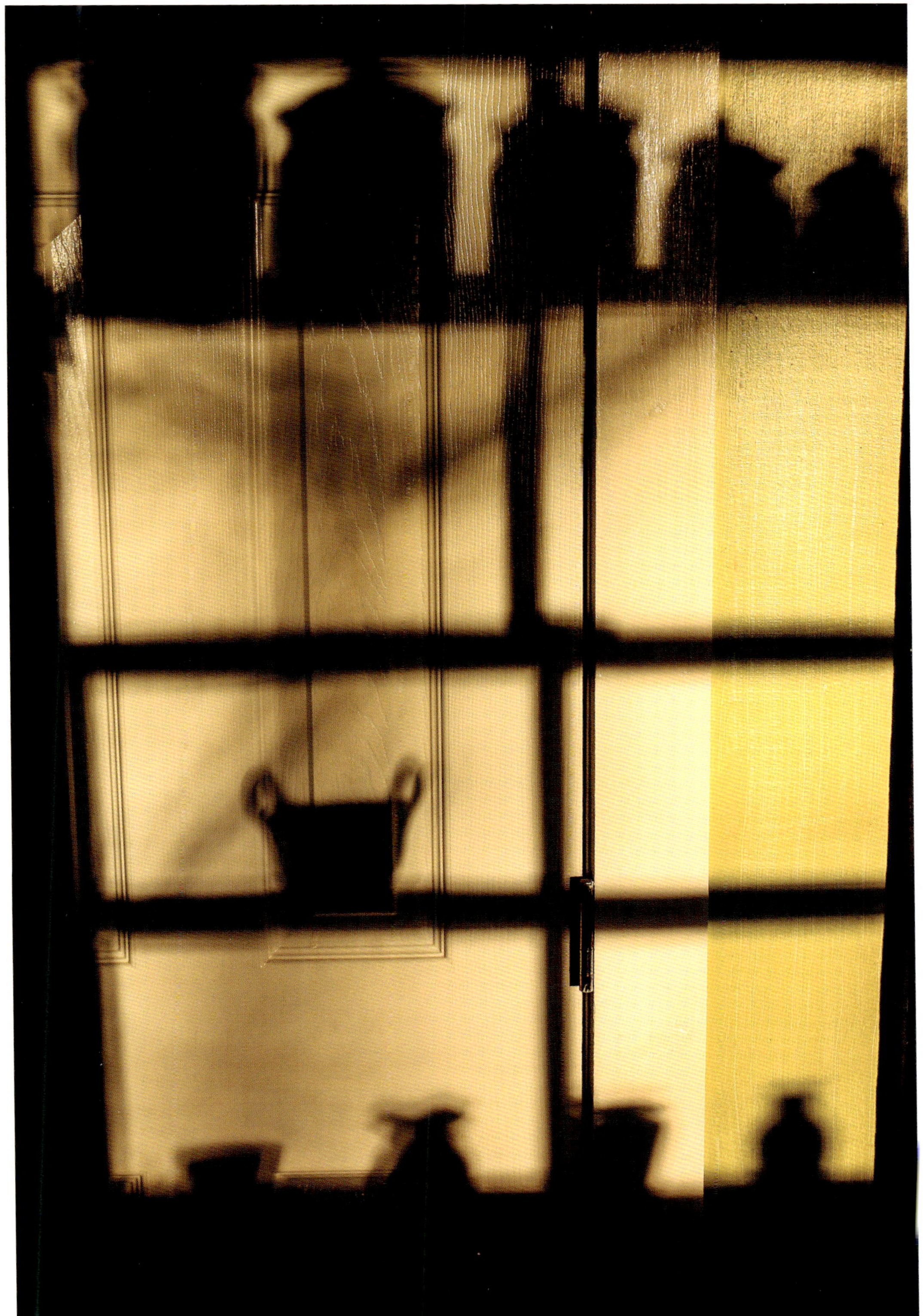

Swear to God
what with Billy's croup
and the baby's cutting teeth
sometimes I'm up all night
baby on the boob
me and Billy and baby
crouching by the kettle in the steam tent

Sometimes I get so tired
my face breaks out all gray
and little red spots

One supper I burned the fish sticks
stank up the kitchen something good
Billy looks at me *Mama!*
so I threw the plates to the floor
and commenced to cry

But that sweet man—
cracks me a beer
scoops up Billy and the baby
winks at me
tells me *We'll mess with this shit later*
puts us in the truck and drives us to the lake

Breathe he tells me
baby breathe
and look at it *just look at it*

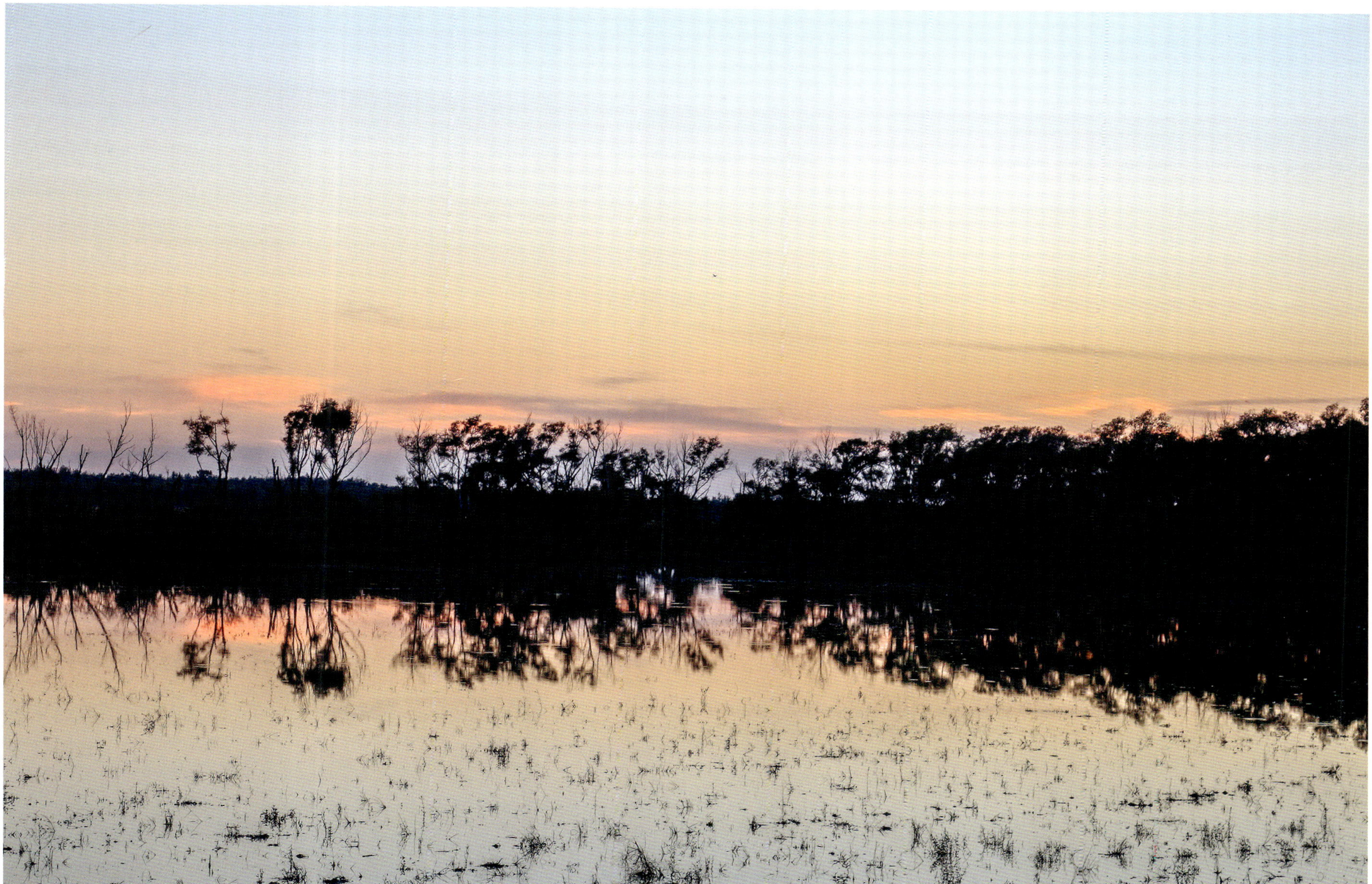

—Oh but still,
in the virgin's bower and all the nameless vines,
cicadas stitch the felty night,
and the Carolina wren tucks deep into her nest,
a shabby, twiggy cup
jammed up against a corner
outside the kitchen door. You turn to me,
sweat-slippery, and I hold you,
stroke your forehead and damp hair,
we drift, and breathe, and fall into sleep,
into this home where we will die.

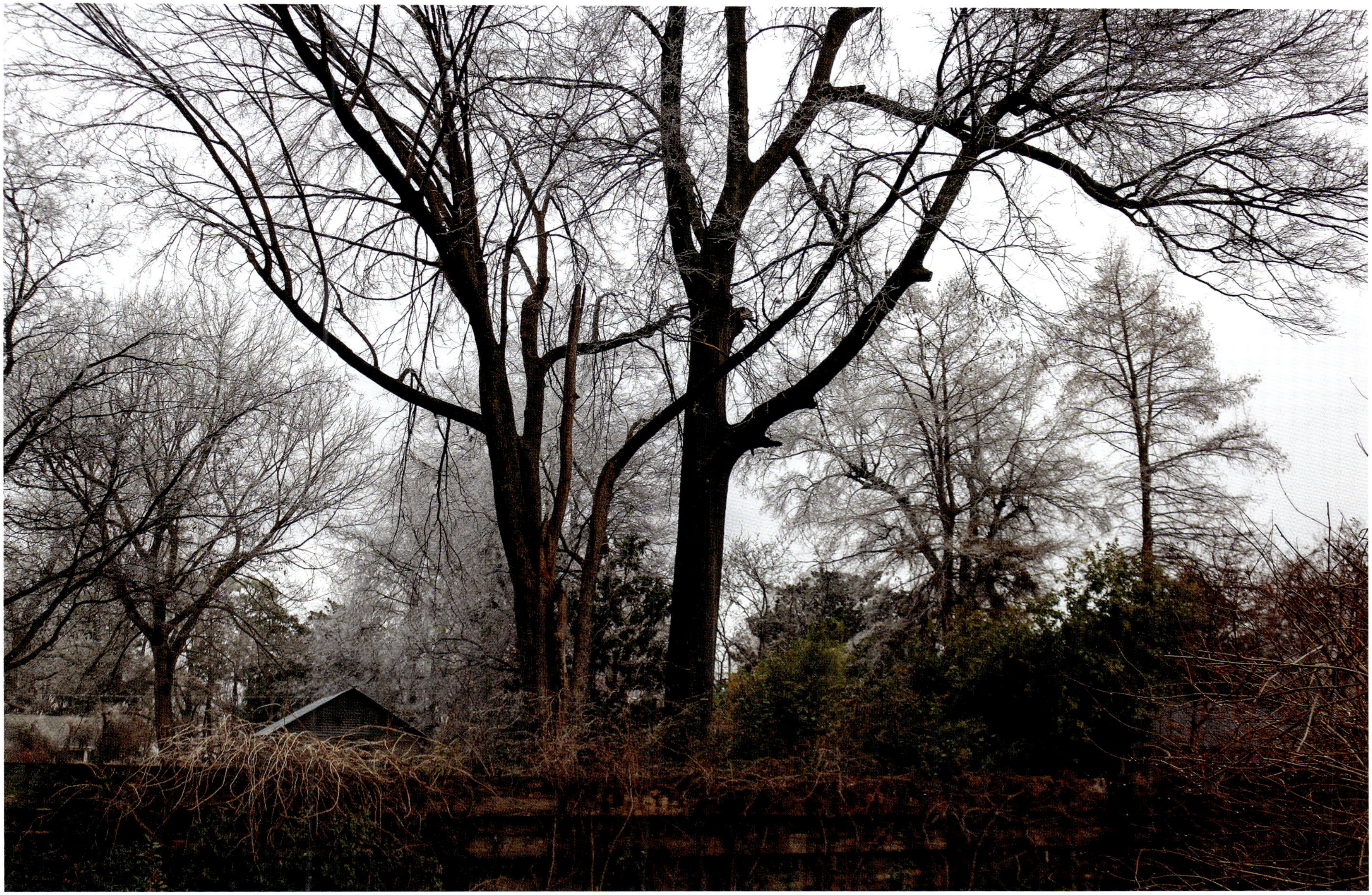

I pulled the rake through stubbly grass

eased it beneath the scarlet crysanthemums'
trailing brittle stems

until my ribs ached and one hip tweaked
and flared with pain

sorted the few pecans

        if they have fallen   windswept   early
        clung to the husk they are rotten

        if the nights have frozen
                        they will be sweet
        the husks will open like stars

                                When I came inside

a housefly labored, trapped
between the screen and window
climbing up, falling down—

        and light hurled through the skies

                        a lifting up
                                an exaltation

        Yea verily
the season is nearly ended

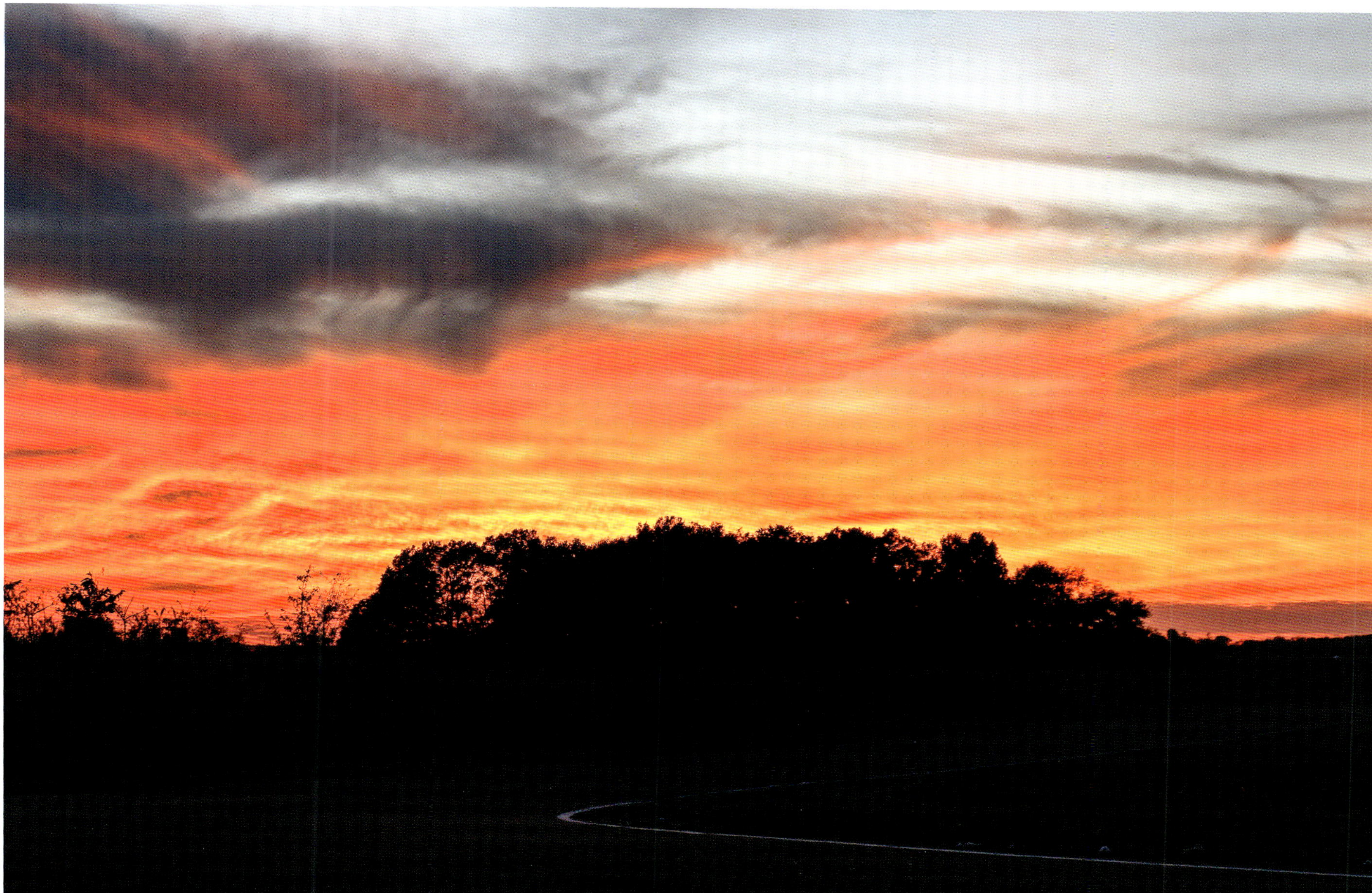

They're not here, are they
        but you want them to be, don't you
                        who are they
                I don't know
but you know
        so tell me what you see

                        eyes like opals
                calm as the saint who watches
        the winds from a hill

        did you love them

                did you kill them

did you spend your whole life missing them

                        nights, they come back
                and take their places

this is how history plays you
                        mountains, empires
        crumble to dust

                red blood flows in their veins again
                        they drag their wet lives
        from the bottom of sleep

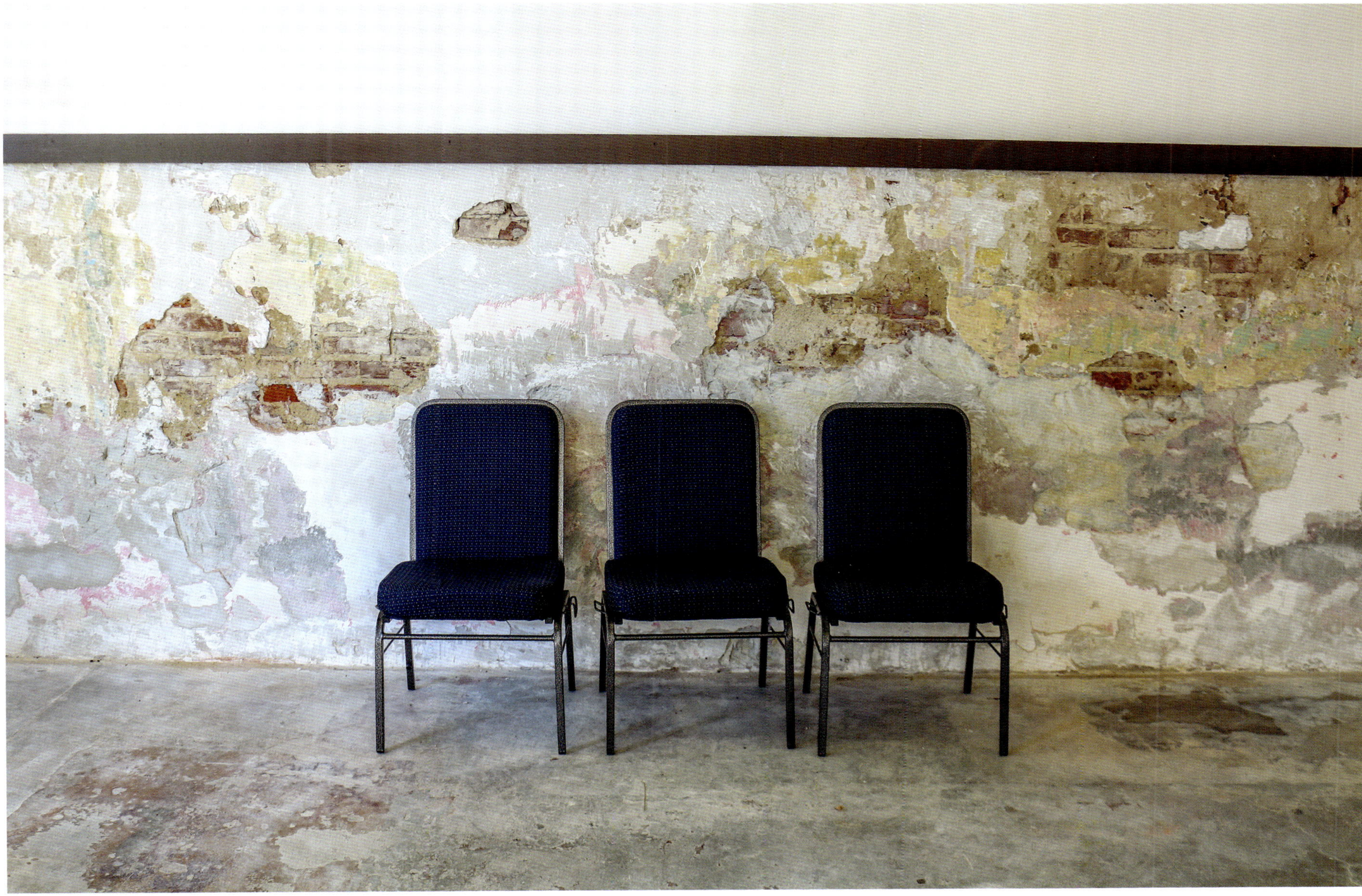

Though they ate in silence
when he turned to her she welcomed him

now as the seasons pass the husk remains

Light filters down
through spiky winterbare trees

Once she laid plates on the table   turned and stooped
to open the heavy oven door

Once he scraped rancid mud from his shoes

Light shines through walls
from which boards are missing

The house
its strawberry-colored roof
picking up pink from the fields   the sky
drenched and pulsing

Light snakes away from the house
in watery furrows

Look
you could follow their paths

You could pick your way gingerly
but what would you find there

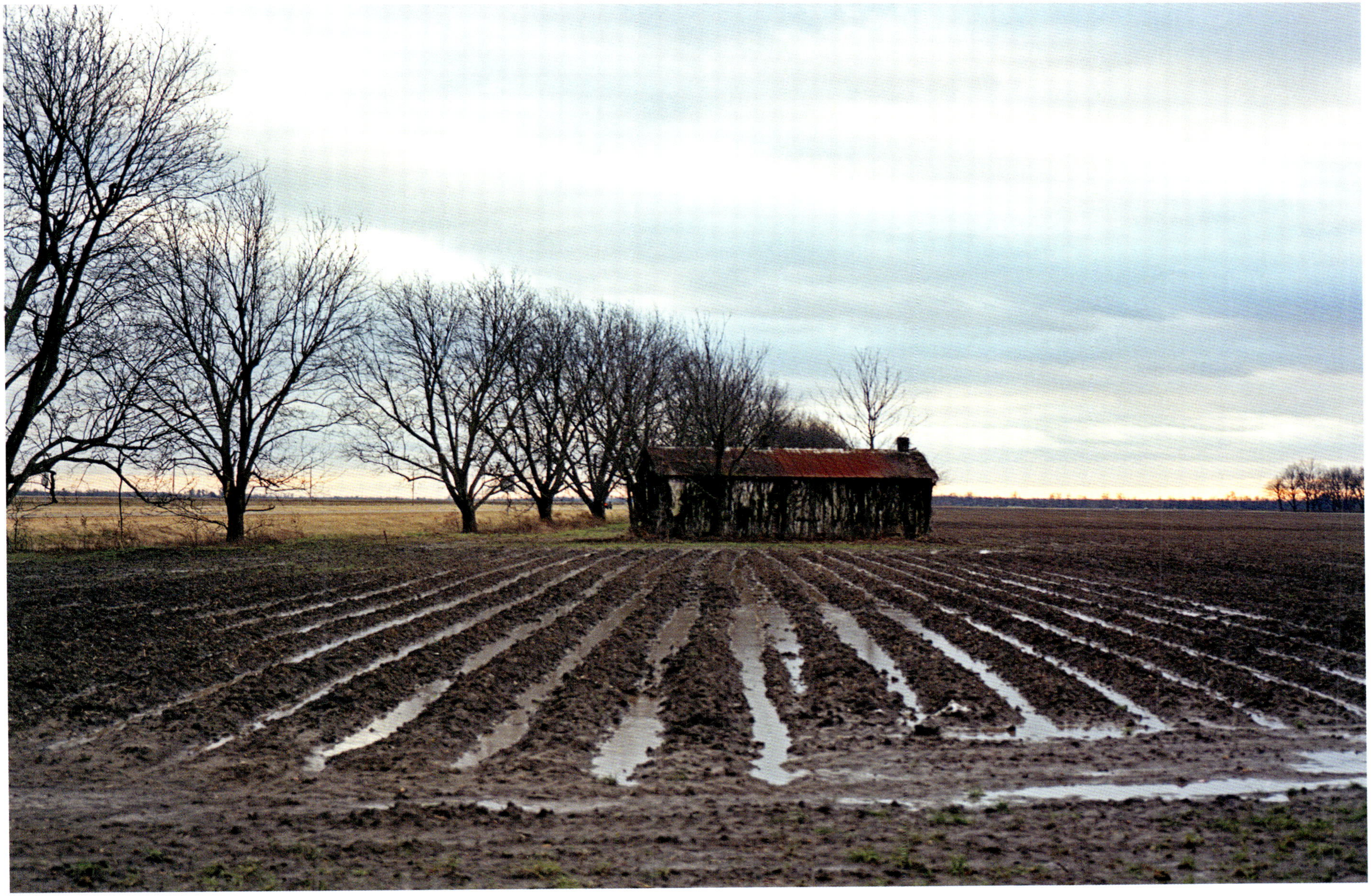

Notes

The characters and voices in *Mississippi* are fictional. Sometimes they intersect with history. The poems do not have titles. Therefore I list them by their first lines, bracketed.

9 [Between two worlds] The boat belonged to Maude's friend Hollan Roberson DeLoach (March 15, 1948-March 15, 2013). I wrote this poem soon after her death.

11 [The heron he come from beyond] The bird in this photograph is an egret but the speaker says it it a heron.

33 [We read these books in 101] This poem is for the girl whose name I do not remember, who was my student twenty-seven years ago when I first was teaching in Mississippi, in honor of her ferocity about family loyalty in *Antigone*.

39 [Sister Laurent made us memorize] The painting described in the poem is by the Mississippi painter Robert Malone.

45 [—And the five o'clock sun] This poem is for my mother and her family.

47 [You stand in Tree, *vrksasana*] *Vrksasana* is the Sanskrit name of the yoga pose called Tree.

51 [I wonder if the chair's still there] This poem is dedicated to the memory of our neighbor, Paul Cavanaugh, who asked for my old wicker chair shortly before his death in December of 2012.

55 [Just for a day] The Mississippi State Penitentiary, also known as Parchman Farm, is the oldest prison and only maximum security prison for men in Mississippi. It is located in Sunflower County in the Delta, southeast of Clarksdale. My colleague Professor Patrick Alexander, whose field is prison literature, has taken me to Parchman, where he is working with Professor Otis Pickett to develop a prison-to-college program, and we have talked about the great lack of opportunity that released prisoners face in Mississippi. Riding with Patrick to Parchman one winter morning, I saw a flock of geese flying over the bare cotton fields.

59 [I do not like snake] This poem is dedicated to two unidentified bodies I read about in 1967, long before I lived in Mississippi—African American boys wearing CORE t-shirts whose murdered bodies were found in the Pearl (or Tallahatchie?) River.

61 [When it commenced it come on fast] For Cora Lee Simpson and her just-born baby, who died together on September 1, 1930. I know nothing about them. Their grave in St. Peter's cemetery, Oxford, haunts me.

67 [He ain't done right to whistle] At the heart of Mississippi's Civil Rights history is Emmett Till, an African American boy murdered on August 28, 1955, at the age of fourteen. He had come from his home in Chicago to visit relatives in the Delta town of Money, Mississippi. Reportedly he spoke to or whistled at twenty-one-year-old Carolyn Bryant, the married proprietor of a small grocery store in Money. Several nights later, Bryant's husband Roy and his half-brother J. W. Milam came and got Till from his great-uncle's house, and took him away to a barn. There they beat him and gouged out one of his eyes, then shot him through the head, weighted his body with a cotton gin fan tied around his neck, and disposed of his body in the Tallahatchie River. Three days later, Till's body was discovered and retrieved. It was prepared for burial in Tutwiler, Mississippi, and returned to his mother in Chicago. There, she insisted on an open casket funeral, insisting that the world see what had been done to her son, and images of Emmett's barely recognizable face were broadcast all around the world. Bryant and Milam were acquitted in court; subsequently, protected from double jeopardy, they admitted their guilt in an interview in *Look* magazine. Emmett Till's death and the worldwide horror that it awoke became a pivotal force in the African American Civil Rights movement. The Money store is now in ruins.

69 [Well you know back then couldn't no] Emmett Till's great-uncle Mose Wright acted with enormous courage when he stood at the trial to identify Bryant and Milam as the men who had taken Till. Nevertheless, the jury took only 67 minutes to acquit.

73 [—*Take that flag down,*] Shortly after Dylan Storm Roof killed nine people at Emanuel African Methodist Episcopal (AME) Church in Charleston, South Carolina, in June 2015, I was at Parchman with Patrick Alexander and Otis Pickett. One of the students in their class, an elderly incarcerated man whose name I do not know, said this about Governor Nikki Haley's decision to take down the Confederate flag shortly after the murders.

75 [I'm scared if I get senile] This poem is for all those, no matter who or where they may be, who wish their memories, brains, and hearts had never been infected with racism.

79 [He's waiting at the crossroads] The legend that Robert Johnson met the Devil at the crossroads, Bob Dylan's song "Man in a Long Black Coat," and Eudora Welty's story "Livvie" get all mixed up together in this poem.

Credits and Acknowledgments

Many thanks to the following publications, in which some of the poems in *Mississippi* have appeared or will appear, sometimes in different versions:

About Place (Black Earth Institute): [Between two worlds], [He comes to your door], and [You stand in Tree].

Bloom: [And the five o'clock sun], [Had me a dog once], [Once we drove to the lake], and [These August afternoons].

Dark Mountain Poetics, Issue Ten: Uncivilised Poetics, ed. Em Strang: [He comes to your door].

Down to the Dark River: An Anthology of Poems about the Mississippi River, ed. Philip C. Kolin and Jack B. Bedell (LSU Press, 2015): [You may not have these cushions] and [He's waiting at the crossroads] (with the title "Spectral").

Heron Tree: [Why do you think you must have something to say] as "Mouna."

ISLE: [Oh but still…], [When it commenced it come on fast] and [I pulled the rake through stubbly grass].

Poetry Salzburg: [Devil each night he come around my door…] and [I'd never stayed in such a place…]

Southern Humanities Review: [He ain't done right to whistle], [I do not like snake], [Sometimes I gaze], [Women what do they want], and [Your hands on my face].

Southampton Review: [I wonder if the chair's still there], [I pulled the rake through stubbly grass], [The heron he comes from beyond], and [Though they ate in silence].

Thinking Continental: Surveying, Exploring and Inhabiting Macro Space, ed. Tom Lynch, Drucilla Wall, and O. Alan Weltzien, University of Nebraska Press, 2017: [Thirty-five years] (with the title "Mississippi Delta Lay Down").

White Rabbit (rpt.): [Why do you think you must have something to say] as "Mouna."

[You may not have these cushions] and [He's waiting at the crossroads] were read and filmed in April 2016 as part of "Mississippi River Dance," the University of Mississippi's performance for National Water Dance, on Mud Island, Memphis, Tennessee.

I am grateful to the Black Earth Institute for their support of this project, and to the Center for the Study of Southern Culture at the University of Mississippi, which exhibited twenty-two of these poems as letterpress broadsides printed by Daniel Uncapher of Ridge & Furrow Press, in Water Valley, Mississippi, with accompanying photographs by Maude Schuyler Clay, in Spring 2016. The exhibition traveled to the Cultural Arts Center, Clarksdale, Mississippi, in October 2016, and to the Ford Center, University of Mississippi, University, Mississippi, in November 2016. At the Ford Center, a performance piece involving six actors and twenty-four poems took place in February 2017.

Many people have helped make this book possible, and to all of them I extend my warmest thanks. The members of my online Wompo workshop gave me innumerable hours of critique and encouragement. Liam Baranauskas, Aziza Barnes, Beth Ann Fennelly, Andrew Freiman, Amie Irwin, Katie Jurkiewicz, and especially Virginia Henry generously provided technical help and critical feedback. CAMAC, the Centre d'Art in Marnay, France, granted me a month-long residency during which I began the book, and the Djerassi Resident Artists Program in Woodside, California granted me a month-long residency during which I completed the book; it was begun and completed in places where I was surrounded by beauty, and I am very grateful. My warmest thanks, too, to Michael McDermott and the Black Earth Institute, and to the University of Mississippi, for generous subventions, and to Bryce Milligan of Wings Press, for his expertise. My love, always, to my family. Most of all, I thank Maude Schuyler Clay, without whose haunting and lovely work this book would not be.

—Ann Fisher-Wirth

Thank you to my family and to all the people who have responded to my photographs over the years. And mainly a huge thank you to Ann Fisher-Wirth for prodding me to do this project, and for allowing me to pair her amazing poetry with my photography.

—Maude Schuyler Clay

About the Photographer

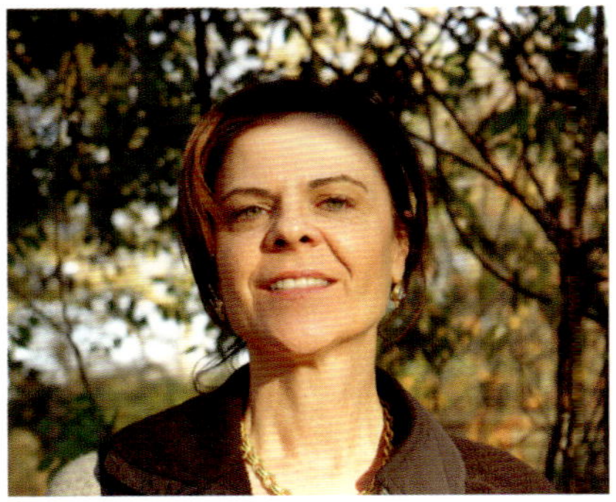

Maude Schuyler Clay was born in Greenwood, Mississippi. After attending the University of Mississippi and the Memphis Academy of Arts, she assisted the photographer William Eggleston. Her photographs have appeared in publications such as *Esquire, Fortune,* and *Vanity Fair,* and are included in the collections of The Museum of Modern Art, The Museum of Fine Arts, Houston, The National Museum for Women in the Arts, and the High Museum, Atlanta, among others.

After working in New York for several years, she returned to live in the Mississippi Delta in 1987. Clay continued her color portrait work, for which she received a Mississippi Arts and Letters Award for Photography. In an artist statement, she wrote, "I prefer to take photographs in the natural low light of early morning or late afternoon, 'in the gloaming,' as the Scots called it—the last rays of eery, orange light that blanket the evening before the sun disappears for the night."

In 1993, she began a series of stark black and white photographs of the Mississippi Delta landscape. The University Press of Mississippi published her widely recognized monograph, *Delta Land,* in 1999, which received another Mississippi Arts and Letters Award in 2000. She was the Photography Editor of the literary magazine, *The Oxford American,* from 1998 to 2002. *Delta Dogs,* with text by Beth Ann Fennelly, and an introduction by Brad Watson, was published by the University of Mississippi Press in 2014. Her most recent book, *Mississippi History,* with a foreword by Richard Ford, was published by Steidl in 2015. She continues to live and work in the Delta.

For more information, go to www.maudeclay.com.

About the Author

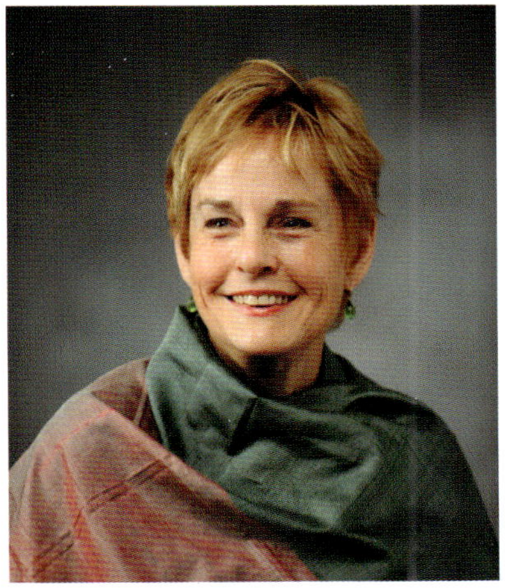

Ann Fisher-Wirth was born in Washington, D. C., and lived as a child in Germany, Pennsylvania, Japan and Berkeley, California. She holds a Ph.D. in English and American literature from Claremont Graduate School. Fisher-Wirth has held Fulbrights to Switzerland and Sweden. She has taught at the University of Mississippi since 1988. Her scholarly work includes *William Carlos Williams and Autobiography: The Woods of His Own Nature* (Penn State University Press, 1989). Known for her poetry's focus on environmental themes and issues, she is a co-editor with Laura-Gray Street of *The Ecopoetry Anthology*, (Trinity University Press, 2013).

Fisher-Wirth's books of poems include *Blue Window* (Archer Books, 2003), *Five Terraces* (Wind Publications, 2005), *Carta Marina* (Wings Press, 2009), and *Dream Cabinet* (Wings Press, 2012), and the chapbooks *The Trinket Poems, Walking Wu-Wei's Scroll, Slide Shows,* and *First, earth.* She has received a *Malahat Review* Long Poem Prize, the Rita Dove Poetry Award, the Mississippi Institute of Arts and Letters Poetry Award, two Mississippi Arts Commission Poetry Fellowships, and fourteen Pushcart nominations. She has been awarded residencies at The Mesa Refuge, Djerassi Resident Artists Program, Hedgebrook, and CAMAC. A fellow of the Black Earth Institute, she was Anne Spencer Poet in Residence at Randolph College in Lynchburg, Virginia, in April 2017.

For more information, go to www. annfisherwirth.com.

Colophon

This first edition of *Mississippi,* with poems by Ann Fisher-Wirth and photographs by Maude Schuyler Clay, has been printed on 70 pound paper containing a percentage of recycled fiber. Titles have been set in Flat Brush type, the text in Adobe Caslon type. All Wings Press books are designed and edited by Bryce Milligan.

This book was made possible by generous subvention grants from the University of Mississippi, Oxford, and the Black Earth Institute.

Wings Press was founded in 1975 by Joanie Whitebird and Joseph F. Lomax, both deceased, as "an informal association of artists and cultural mythologists dedicated to the preservation of the literature of the nation of Texas." Publisher, editor and designer since 1995, Bryce Milligan is honored to carry on and expand that mission to include the finest in American writing—meaning all of the Americas, without commercial considerations clouding the decision to publish or not to publish.

Wings Press publishes multi-cultural books, chapbooks, ebooks, recordings and broadsides intended to enlighten the human spirit and enliven the mind. Everyone ever associated with Wings has been or is a writer; we recognize writing as a transformational art form capable of changing the world, primarily by allowing us to glimpse something of each other's souls. We believe that good writing is innovative, insightful, and interesting. But most of all it is honest. As Bob Dylan put it, "To live outside the law, you must be honest."

Likewise, Wings Press is committed to treating the planet itself as a partner. Thus the press uses as much recycled material as possible, from the paper on which books are printed to the boxes in which they are shipped.

As Robert Dana wrote in *Against the Grain,* "Small press publishing is personal publishing. In essence, it's a matter of personal vision, personal taste and courage, and personal friendships." Welcome to our world.

On-line catalogue and ordering: www.wingspress.com • Wings Press titles are distributed to the trade by the Independent Publishers Group: www.ipgbook.com • European distribution by Gazelle Book Services: www.gazellebookservices.co.uk